The Sociology of Light

CONVERGENCE IN
ART, SCIENCE, AND RELIGION

Calvin Moore

Chadwick Books

To Dorothy.

Acknowledgments

I would like to thank Simona Epuran and Donna Maurer for their years of friendship, valuable support and feedback as I pursued the ideas contained in these essays. Simona was the first to engage me with true interest in these ideas. She actively read and commented upon early experimental essays. Her intellectual contributions have proved invaluable to the completion of this work. Donna has been a friend and advisor for many years and, to my good fortune, a professional editor. I extend my gratitude to her for her support.

Contents

"Light! More Light!"
Goethe

Introduction

The following set of essays on the sociology of light can be thought of as an intersection of the sociology of art and the sociology of religion in which the concept of light – an essential element of both – is extracted for analysis as to both its social construction and its social effects. The overall objective of the essays is to provoke discussion as to how differences in conceptualizations of light in art and religion among Eastern, Western, Middle Eastern and sub-Saharan African cultures may have contributed to variations in the social and technological development among these respective cultural regions of the world.

Art and religion represent some of the oldest human responses to the phenomenon of light. Art altered the material world to project light into the consciousness of human subjects in such a manner that it acts as a social force. According to Max Weber, art contributed to the rationalization and stylization of the form of humans, their material productions and their environments. Art has the power to move human subjects and can thus be employed as a tool of social control. It was thus useful for the class of priests seeking to impose rational order upon discordant human interactions in society. Light is therefore a central element of many of the world's religions. Hinduism, Buddhism, Christianity and Islam have all yielded intense discourses on the subject of light in the course of their development and contain many practices that are either manifestly or latently directed towards light.

Beyond art and religion, there are many fields of human intellectual endeavor for which light is a primary subject: Light-related themes pervade philosophical thought and literature is infused with countless metaphors surrounding the idea of light. Light is a primary subject of many of the natural sciences – not only do cosmology, optics, physics, biochemistry and related fields of study take on light as a subject-matter, all the natural sciences employ light as an essential tool in the quest for the truth about existence. Modern technologies are premised upon the dissection and manipulation of light energy in the pursuit of human objectives.

Truth is indeed light: All objects in the world are presented to the human subject through the senses as reflections of radiant energy from those objects to the subject. The human senses absorb radiant energy from the environment and transmit it as an organized series of electromagnetic waves to the brain for interpretation and response. Visible light accounts for the vast majority of the radiant energy that mediates human interaction with the world and thus is the dominant means by which we learn about the world.

The essays contained in this work are written to demonstrate that the conceptualization of light by human societies is a significant source of human motivation. They draw attention to how societal variations in discourses on light may contribute to variations in societal development. Taken together, the essays also offer a means of reconciling surface contradictions between discourses in religion and the sciences and suggest a method by which both sets of discourses can be integrated into a singular narrative about the primacy of light in the efforts of humans to understand their existence and to fully express their being.

These ideas may be perceived as reductionist and they are: Existence is examined purely as a product of interactions between light and matter – the material substance of the world - in which the patterns of light produced by the interactions are absorbed into a mysterious "consciousness" in the process of human experience. Human intellectual disciplines seek to understand the underlying laws that govern these interactions and to use that understanding to shape light-material relations in a manner that achieves societal aims. Culture establishes and enforces the norms of light-matter interaction that derive from these intellectual endeavors. These norms are expressed not only in the fields of religion and art, but also in the countless aesthetically-informed cultural productions through which the human experience is intentionally framed.

Chapter 1, "What Is Art?" considers the nature of art's function as a guide in the quest for human liberation. The sociology of art of Georg Simmel is introduced to present the question as to what it is that humans are attempting to achieve through their artistic reordering of the world.

Chapter 2, "The Evolution of Art Form" describes a walk through a corridor in an art museum that revealed a progression of freedom of movement from the formal, linear rigidity of ancient Egyptians through the fluidity of relations inherent in Eastern art, to the infinitely extended curve expressed in Greek and subsequent Western art. The essay closes with the suggestion that African art extends movement along an even greater dimension of freedom and expresses the ultimately liberating lines of force that underlie the modern art movement.

Chapter 3, "The Mechanics of "Up" proposes that the liberation quest at the heart of both art and religion stems primarily from the human desire to overcome the downward pull of gravity that ultimately leads to the death and dispersion of the living body. Art and religion are viewed as meditations upon a quest for "up" that has parallels in the organization of the organic molecules that are the foundation of life on earth.

The quest for upness in ancient Egypt is contrasted with Eastern conceptions and mechanisms for obtaining the desired upness. Of technological significance is the emphasis in the Egyptian aesthetic order on the ideal of upward thrust as the source of liberation in contrast to the more horizontal dispersion of light energy expressed in Eastern physical and metaphysical systems of thought. The emphasis on upward thrust was absorbed into western systems of religious, philosophical and scientific thought and provided the West with an edge in the pursuit of the efficient forward momentum that is the foundational principle of modern technology.

Chapter 4, "Western Light and the Liberation Quest", distinguishes pre-Renaissance from post-Renaissance conceptualizations of light in art and religion. While the early Christian and medieval project for the soul was focused primarily on organizing light in a manner that sent it upwards for union with God in heaven, the post-Renaissance intellectual endeavor came to focus increasingly on the scientific dissection of light with an effort that was focused upon efficiently directing light energy through the world rather than up to God. The shift in focus resulted in the development of an ever-increasingly nuanced mechanical system for reordering light-material relations in the world. The result is the production of the power that is necessary for the pursuit of human freedom.

Chapter 5, "From Diamond in Water to Water in Diamond: The Evolution of the Western Soul" traces changes in the West in how the act of perception occurs in the human subject. Two conceptions of idealized universal bodies are contrasted: The first is that of a body with a perfectly reflecting (carbon) diamond center whose absorption and reflection of light energy into the human soul powers bodily movements. The second and more contemporary conceptualization is a body characterized as complex electrical circuitry composed of electrons distributed through the water that constitutes most of the body's substance. While carbon atoms still provide the primary structure for the living body, electrons become the means through which the human subject interacts with a fluid "consciousness" instead of the classical Christian soul.

Chapter 6, "Totem, Light and Power" considers the origins and functions of totems as organizing forces in early human societies. The functions of totems are traced from their initial roles as objects initially designed to constrain the many spirits that were thought to be responsible for movement in the world to objects that served as the foundations of information systems designed to the control behavior of group members in a society. Religions are conceived as totemic systems. The light-ordered objectives of the dominant world religions – Hinduism, Judeo-Christianity, Buddhism and Islam - in the organization of their totemic orders are compared.

In chapter 7, "Structural Foundations of Culture: Square Frames, Redundancy and Luminosity," the foundational rules are considered by which light is structured by the various cultures of the world in the pursuit of human aims.

Chapter 8, "Culture, Light, and Freedom" offers a methodology for studying cultural variations in light-material relations. A procedure is set forth for collecting and analyzing internet images that are illustrative of a culture's orientation to light. The representation of serpents and dragons in Egypt, the East, and the West are analyzed for what they reveal about the ideational orientations of the social and material order of the cultures that produced them.

Throughout the work is the infusion of the discourses of art and religion with those discourses on light that have developed in the western sciences. In the tradition of the structuralist intellectual movement that dominated the late twentieth-century human sciences, the goal of this work is not to differentiate the various human discourses on light, but to determine the foundational rules from which all of these discourses spring and by which they are all ultimately unified.

1

What is Art?

Georg Simmel defines culture as life producing certain forms "in which it expresses and realizes itself: works of art, religions, sciences, technologies, laws, and innumerable others".[i] The common denominator of these forms is the shifting of the building blocks of life, that is to say, the materials that define physical reality, in a manner that "expresses and realizes" life. Behind these material transformations are the unseen forces, both natural and ideational, that are responsible for such shifts wherein the ideational forces for the evolution of form are products of human reflection upon the underlying natural laws that determine form.

Simmel notes the eternal conflict between realized form and the energy of life that is constantly destroying form through unceasing change. Humanity is always torn between these two conceptions of Being and is satisfied with the supremacy of neither as each offers a form of liberation that is the antithesis of the other: The idea of eternal form, or Being, offers freedom from dissolution, while the dynamic forces of change, or ever Becoming, offers the possibility of ultimately liberating movement. Yet each offers a form of non-freedom as well: The idea of the eternal form presents the possibility of a static and potentially stagnant form of existence where the possibilities of Being are never fully realized while change denies eternity to the being and keeps it in constant fear of dissolution. Eternal being and the freedom to creatively and endlessly express thus seem to be contradictory aims that ever divide the human spirit. The attempt to mediate this duality results the driving dynamic of human culture.

The outcome of the conflict is that while life takes on form, no form can fully express life. Simmel thus states that "whenever life expresses itself, it desires to express only itself; thus it breaks through any form which would be superimposed on it by some other reality."[ii] In speaking of the form of a painting, he states, "The established phenomenon, the painting, does of course have a form. But according to the artist's intention, the form represents only a necessary evil."[iii] The artist takes upon himself the task of representing the experience of life within a medium, knowing full well the inadequacy of the materials with which he works – the materials through which he presents his representations through his consciously-directed hands can only incompletely portray the life force in all its complex, unfolding evolution. The artist is compelled to make the attempt to impose a form upon life, knowing that ultimately, his expression of life will be incomplete.

To Simmel, the desire to more completely express life through art explains the shift towards abstraction in modern art; modern artists awakened to the realization that they could never fully capture the life force by adhering to the classical rules of aesthetics. Those rules bound them to external representations of objects with a view towards the beautiful. Life, however, is much more complex than those representations could ever produce. Form not only exists in a multitude of levels beneath the surface of those representations, but also expresses itself dynamically in both space and time. Modern art thus sought to better express the multi-dimensionality of objects in the world that was impossible to achieve by adhering to rules of classical aesthetics.

The artists therefore had to go beyond beauty and into the exploration of forms in which beauty and ugliness did not matter. They had to attempt to reveal essences of represented objects, and those essences had to encompass not only those eternal forms that classical artists tried to freeze on paper, but also the dynamic forces through which life was expressing itself. This new form of expression pushed freedom of movement to new limits by allowing the components of form, the underlying structures of form, to shift about on the canvas in the manner similar to which life seemed to be constantly shifting its component structures in it unceasing desire to express itself anew.

Abstract art is a quest for liberation. Simmel states that "the desire for completely abstract art among some sectors of modern youth may stem from passion for an immediate and unrestrained (nackten) expression of self."[iv] It is indeed about self-expression, a self-expression that the youth of which he spoke could more and more afford because of the liberation from want, disease, and arbitrary death that had long plagued prior civilizations of humans. In this epoch is an unfolding desire for individuality, an unwillingness to accept objective form, for to do so would "dilute one's vitality by freezing it into the mold of something already dead."[v]

Simmel thus addresses in this essay fundamental questions of the meaning and purpose of life, and how meaning and purpose is expressed through culture. Like others before him, his logic takes him to the ultimate goals of being as consisting of both the desire to exist and to the need to express that existence. These two goals, however, contain some inherent contradiction, because expression requires dissolution of form - forms must be destroyed if new forms are to come to be in the process of expression. The destruction of form in turn perpetrates the fear of dissolution without return.

In the case of humans, we are pulled by desires that are both complementary and contradictory: One desire is to be; the other is to create. Inherent in each form is the destruction of the other. The resulting dynamic is the driving force of change.

----

[i]Etzkorn, Peter. Georg Simmel on the conflict in modern culture. New York: Teacher's College Press. p. 11.

[ii]Simmel, Georg. 1972. *Georg Simmel on individuality of social forms.* Chicago: University of Chicago Press. p. 382.

[iii]Ibid.

[iv]Ibid, p. 384.

[v]Ibid, p. 385.

Chapter Two

The Evolution of Art Form

The following essay was prompted by a visit to the Carnegie Museum of Art in Pittsburgh, Pennsylvania. There is a general organization to most comprehensive art museums, though with significant variation. I like to treat my museum visits as a walk through time and human history, and I find that the organization of most major museums facilitates that. To me, art museums represent a very elite world view; they are the result of the upper-class world collecting what it perceives to be the most powerful reflections upon the human experience through time and then presenting the human experience in its most ideal light. When a cultural artifact is said to be of "museum quality," that means that it is the highest possible representation of its kind that a culture can produce.

Art museums are where art and artifacts are meticulously and beautifully arranged in a manner that imposes meaning and significance to the events that compose humanity's unfolding narrative. Inside a museum, one can literally walk through thousands of years of human history, across continents and cultures surveying the outputs of each society's material productions by its most talented and deeply reflective members. I can therefore expect in a large museum visit for my body to move and my consciousness to flow through highly stylized snapshots of the histories and cultures of ancient Egypt, Greece, Rome, India, China and Japan. I should also find representations of Oceanic, pre-Colombian American and African art and culture.

In these sections, one will find the wide variety of cultural artifacts that these societies have produced, from functional, everyday utensils to furniture, architecture, sculpture, and paintings, with oil European and American oil paintings usually representing the centerpieces of the entire collection. Visits to art museums over time yield to the viewer a sense of the idealized forms produced by a wide variety of cultures over time. The accumulated experience of museum visits over the years thus presents the opportunity for an analysis of underlying patterns and structural commonalities through which fundamental rules of human-generated form may be discerned.

This essay is a commentary upon the organization of just a particular hallway in the Carnegie that ran between several larger galleries but was still decorated with art and sculpture. The passageway is memorable because it allowed me to traverse over three thousand years of history and the breadth of several continents in very short order. It began with ancient Egyptian art, followed by Eastern art - largely Indian and Chinese, after which followed examples of the Greco-Roman tradition. I then exited the Greco-Roman gallery and entered a gallery African art containing primarily masks and sculptures, after which I made a left turn out of the long hall of galleries into a large room that appropriately began the modern art section.

I struck by the fact that as the walk proceeded from the Egyptian gallery to the African, a new dimension of movement appeared to be successively added in each room. The progression made it all the more appropriate that the curators placed the African art section at the end of the hall, after the Greeks and before the turn into the modern art section instead of before the Egyptians in a manner that would have relegated it to most "primitive" status. This essay is a commentary upon the order of this arrangement in light of the above essay concerning the relationship between art and the human liberation quest.

Egypt

Art has long been a significant social force in the patterning of material forms and appears to have served the function of idealizing the human form in Egyptian culture. Weber suggests that the impulse for such stylization may have it roots in religion and the desire of a class of priests to impose constraints upon the human body. Art, however, eventually moved beyond religion and assumed an independent authority over form. Its ability to stylize form gave it the power to "take over the function [of religion] in this worldly salvation." Art not only provides salvation from the routines of life, it also produces stylizations and forms that set the foundation for the rationalization of life. Art can thus provide the foundation for rational order, which in turn increases the predictability of relations among social members and between social bodies and their environment.

Consider the familiar diagram of the progression of the hominid form from the curved spine to the ape to the rigid spine of Homo erectus. While the succession of images of the human form may make the progression seem natural and even inevitable, some consideration must be given to the facts that the linear human form is socially constructed, that its development was not even, and that there thus arose members of a group who embraced the idea sooner than later. These innovators of form then imposed it upon others as an enforced norm through the application of social power.

Certain forms come to mind when one thinks of representations of the human body in ancient Egyptian art. Bodies are generally presented in flat, angular poses. They tend to be rigid, square, and stiff. Torsos are drawn or sculpted as rectangular blocks with arms extending downwards from vertical shoulders in sharp angles towards narrow waists and equally rigid legs. When a figure is sitting, it is usually with the head and torso forming a horizontal line that connects to the horizontally positioned waist and thighs, upon which the lower legs descend horizontally at another sharp, ninety-degree angle. Noteworthy for later discussion is the human form when viewed from the side expresses the movement of the electromagnetic wave through which light energy is expressed and is poised in the direction of upness.

There is minimal muscle definition in Egyptian figures; body and facial features tend to be portrayed in blocked, geometric forms. If one were to imagine any of the figures moving, movement would be very robotic in nature. I am sure that Egyptians did not move that way in real life - their bodies were endowed with the same flexibility as our bodies are today. Nonetheless, one can see in Egyptian art a desire to "perfect" human bodies and actions by idealizing rigid, formal, straight, square and predictable relations among the parts that compose their bodies.

Egyptian productions epitomize the flat, square, rigid formality through which the nobility, with the assistance of the priesthood, sought to impose order upon both their subjects and the natural world. It was likely the nobility who first realized that standing straight upwards over stooped individuals made them feel more imposing and powerful. They also came to understand the inherent efficiency and predictability embodied in the straight lines and ninety-degree angles that would come to dominate their art and architecture. More labor power, that power that was necessary to transform the material world, could be extracted from the human body if it moved along a series of complementary planes. For the Egyptians, then, the rigid body was liberation from the chaotic and hence destructive and excessive energy-consuming movements of the uncoordinated horde-like movements from which civilization was trying to rise.

The power of a civilization ultimately rests in its ability to organize and coordinate the movements of its social members, whether it is for war or for economic production. The Egyptians were one of the first great civilizations to achieve such coordinated organization on scales previously unrealized in human history. The rigid, formal structures of Egyptian art are both reflections and precipitators of that outcome.

The East

I am describing a walk through a long, narrow gallery at the Carnegie Museum of Art in which I also traversed over three thousand years of human history. Something happened when I left the Egyptian room and entered the Eastern gallery. It is as if another dimension of movement is opened and it was very self-evident and powerful at the time. The difference is the result of the addition of three dimensions of movement and material organization to the artwork in the gallery: curvature, redundancy, centeredness and stillness.

Curvature

Eastern art introduced the concept of a gently flowing curve that was not a dominant feature of the Egyptian art. That is not to say that Eastern art originated these concepts, a fact that may have been more evident if there had been included between the Egyptian and Eastern galleries a gallery of ancient Assyrian or other Middle Eastern art. The gallery of Eastern art demonstrated, however, the exploitation of the fullest potential of the curve and redundancy in art, particularly since Middle Eastern art, largely for religious reasons, largely ultimately abandoned the exploration of the human form's potential. Middle Eastern art provides a conceptual pathway to Eastern art, where instead of the rigid, pyramidal, hierarchical, obelisk-shaped structures of Egypt, the dominant order shifts to one of smooth, flowing curves and radiating circles. The dominance of the curve over the straight in the representation of form produces new possibilities for free movement and organization of materials and bodies and thus allows for more complex interactions of objects and materials in space.

The integration of the circle to Eastern art also produced new possibilities of unity and completeness. The Egyptian conception of the world is embodied in a triangular, hierarchical order that is pointed at the top, symbolizing the position in the hierarchy of the Pharaoh as being closest to the sun, and has a wide flat base to accommodate the lowest elements the social order. The social and material order is thus triangular in form as idealized in the Great Pyramids.

Eastern metaphysical systems incorporated the circle into their expressions of form and created the possibility of an idealized body as having a center from which radiated animating light, just as a circle has a center from which may radiate light to touch all its outer parts. The Eastern body is not, then, one of the rectangular blocked bodies that compose Egyptian society. Egyptian bodies possess no individuality or distinctiveness but only serve as parts in the composition of the whole pyramid of Egyptian society. The Eastern body, in contrast, is whole and complete in itself. It has a center and a periphery and can maintain its form as long as the light can shine unimpeded between its interior and surface. The quest for an efficient exchange of light energy between the center and periphery of the idealized body thus defines the enlightenment project of the East. This idealized form is to be contrasted with the rigid, pyramid-shaped body that is idealized in Egyptian art.

The major Eastern religions and ethical systems - Hinduism, Buddhism and Confucianism, teach individuals that whether they exist low or high in the hierarchy of society, they may find satisfaction in their position because if they seek the enlightened path that accords wholeness to their being, they are nonetheless equal to all other beings. Understanding that, individuals can find satisfaction in fulfilling whatever roles that society has accorded them while contributing to a universal harmony in the process that further enhances their freedom in the world. The outcome is an idealized structure of both the individual and social body that is strikingly different from that which is suggested by Egyptian aesthetic ideals.

These ideals are made conceptually possible because of the preeminence of the idea of curved fluidity of the material world and the existence of a universal light to which that material world seeks harmonious relation though an efficiently organized flow between the body's center and its periphery. Light becomes the source of the body's power to align itself with the fluid world. The Eastern ideal of freedom thus becomes the ability of the body to accommodate and join with the watery flow of Universal Being, or the One of which all individualized components of the world are a part. Egyptians, on the other hand, viewed the fluidity of existence as a source of chaos from which the human subject could be liberated only through the imposition of rigid, formality that was premised upon straight rather than curved lines of force. The Egyptian ideal thus represents a liberation from curvature rather than liberation through curvature that was the ideal of the East. Yoga and martial arts could have never developed in ancient Egypt. Both disciplines rely upon the absolute fluidity of body relations rather than the rigidity imposed by Egyptian metaphysics.

Eastern philosophers were as aware as are modern thinkers of the problem of the body. Experience taught them that there were many forces in the world that can disrupt the flow of life energy within the body. Metaphysical systems evolved as attempted solutions to this fundamental problem. One solution was to organize the surrounding forces of the world in as harmonious fashion as possible so that they facilitated rather than disrupted the flow of energy that powered the body. Harmonious body/world interactions thus became the existential goal to pursue in the East. The goal was pursued both through movement and non-movement. Practices such as yoga, tai chi and the martial arts gave the body the flexibility to interact fluidly and harmoniously with one's environment; meditation practices stilled the elements of the body to annihilate all resistance of the body to the flow of the universal one through the body. All these practices relied upon the premise that fluid relations governed existence and the ideal human form and were driven by a desire to accommodate rather than resist the watery flow of universal being.

Redundancy

We also in Eastern art encounter an increased emphasis relative to Egyptian art on redundancy – that is to say that space begins to take on the possibility of infinite divisibility in Eastern art forms. Redundancy is the ability to reproduce geometric forms in space in a manner that allows the form to maintain its integrity but to expand or collapse in size and repetition to theoretically infinite degrees. Spatial relations become more complex; many more planes and lines of force are represented in the same size spaces than were capable in Egyptian art. There is a more refined mastery of space such that greater quantities of distinguishable objects and parts can be inserted into spaces. Object representations become far more detailed than were possible in Egyptian culture. Individual strands of hair and detailed musculature in representation of bodies and greater quantities of individual objects all lend a complexity to object relations that seemed inconceivable in the Egyptian gallery.

Centeredness and Stillness

Another observation as to Eastern systems before I leave the gallery: The incorporation of the circle into the metaphysics also allowed for development of the concept of stillness. Stillness implies centeredness, which is a possibility made much more difficult by the fluid nature of body relations. A circle has both a center and a periphery, and it allows for the contemplation of a perfect set of relations between the center and its outer parts. If the radiance of light from the center of a body powers the being, that radiance must flow efficiently and without interruption from the center to the periphery and back. For the exchange to be eternal, there must be perfect exchange of between the exterior and the interior of the body such that there is no loss of energy in the process.

In such a system, the ultimate source of power is the absolute center from which energy proceeds through the body to its outermost layers and then turns back towards the center. The center of the body produces power by the convergence of energy upon from other surfaces that form the body. It is in this regard that the concept of "stillness" becomes important: All the energy that leave a body's center to power the body must, upon its return to the center, strike a precisely central point simultaneously so as to produce the necessary explosive reaction that has the power to return to the body's outer edges and back again. There must be no lost or displaced energy in the process. The timing and positioning of the returning energy as it converges on the center of the body is critical as the convergence is the central rejuvenating and realigning moment in the system's operation.

As a result of the derivation of this system of the physics of the universal body, Eastern metaphysical systems presented the problem of the human body as an off-centeredness that prevented the efficient convergence of energy at the body's center to produce an efficient and hence eternal flow of energy through the body's material parts. Bodily existence could not be eternally maintained because of this problem. The solution was thus a realignment of the body's forces with its perfect center so as to re-establish the life-sustaining relationship between the body's center and its constituent parts.

Stillness allows for the convergence of energy upon a central point in the body a manner that achieves life-giving radiance and is thus a powerful concept in Eastern metaphysics and religion. Buddha sat still under a tree until he was enlightened. When he was enlightened, light flowed from his center through his body and all parts of his body were organized in perfect harmony with the whole of being. Enlightenment removed all resistances between Buddha's body and the world and in that moment, he achieved perfectly fluid and harmonious relationship with the world that surrounded his body. To do so, however, he had to establish that still point in the center of his being so that energy could converge upon that point and radiate perfectly outwards. It was only then that he was united with the Universal One, in which the body melts away and joins the flowing of the universal waters.

The Eastern concept of freedom is to be distinguished from the Egyptian ideal of resisting and rising above the flow of the waters through the rigid form of the pyramid. The Eastern concept of freedom consists of using one's inner energy to adjust perfectly to the flow of the waters; either one moves freely with and through the waters or one sits still and allows the waters of the universal one to flow through and annihilate the body's resistances. In either case, the concept of curvature is integrated into rather than separated from the Eastern concept of the body.

The Greeks

Let us exit the Eastern world and move forward into the Greek gallery, where we see even more liberating forms of movement represented. Upon entering the room, one sees that there is indeed something about the representations of bodies, materials, and forms in space in this gallery that does not exist in the Eastern gallery. As noted, Eastern systems placed great emphasis upon balance, symmetry and centeredness – Eastern figures of power were always exactly in the center of their surroundings; the world revolved around them in perfect harmony. Eastern metaphysicians were afraid of placing a body in the constellation in a position that was not balanced on the opposite side of the center in equal strength.

The Greek world, like the Eastern world, incorporates the fluidity of curvature and the up-seeking power of rigidity in an exploration of all possibilities of being, but the relations are far more dynamic among the Greeks; the Greeks were not afraid to experiment with kinetic relations that placed the center of a body away from the center of a work – a central figure might be placed to the left or right of center but objects in space are arranged around that central figure so as to maintain the overall balance of the presentation in the square that frame that forms the outer parameters of the work.

We see the concentration of power in parts of the system that are away from the center, and which present the possibility of the exercise of power that is not designed to maintain an overall centered harmony, but that presents the possibility of obliquely directed lines of thrust - movement of force in directions that defy the constraints imposed upon movement in the Egyptian and Eastern systems – away from the straight upness that is the Egyptian ideal and not radiating from the center in conformity with all other lines of force as required in Eastern art. In both the Egyptian and Eastern scenarios, a balanced equilibrium is maintained and neither culture could imagine positioning individual bodies in a manner that upset that balance. The Greeks dared to thrust the lines of their bodies along diagonals in a manner that suggested an infinite extension of the body into space and hence no possibility that it would eventually curve around and reunite harmoniously with the whole as commanded in Eastern art. In this manner, the Greeks introduced the concept of a space that expanded infinitely outwards in contradiction to the idea that all space was ultimately contained by the circle.

No Greek sculpture epitomizes the new direction of movement offered by the Greeks like the statue of Laocoön. If one follows the thrust of Laocoön's body as well as that of other bodies in the sculpture, you see them extending outwards at oblique angles from the center that never suggest the possibility of their lines of force curving back inwards where it must eventually converge at the work's center. The Greeks introduce the possibility of the infinitely extended line of force in their representations of the body.

While the gallery that I walked through on that day did not contain this famous statue, Laocoön's form pervaded all representations of the body in the Greco-Roman statues, painted vases, and architectural carvings. No two bodies ever moved along parallel lines of force. Each moved along a gently curving path in its own unique direction thrusting off into infinity.

I have described above how the sitting Egyptian body when viewed from the sides expresses the progression in space of light as an electromagnetic wave – a set of three lines that meet at ninety-degree angles at the knees and lower torso. This idealized body is the Egyptian ideal of upward movement – straight and formal: The lines of force move straight upwards from the feet to the knees, straight across to the lower torso and straight upwards to the head. In contrast, the ninety-degree angles are softened into the idealized Greek body to form two gentle curves that make the body appear to be swimming diagonally towards infinity in its own unique direction rather than moving upward and forward like a rigid set of stairs.

The Egyptians were afraid of particularity and individuality while Eastern thinkers allowed greater expression of individuality than the Egyptians, though always as part of an integrated and harmonized whole. The Greeks pushed individual freedom to its limits while maintaining an ultimate belief in the power of the human will to remain in control of its relationship with the world. All bodies in Greek art appear to be pushing the boundaries of the frame that encloses them rather than finding their proper place within it. Acute individuality of form is the outcome.

An example is the Greek representation of human hair in its sculptures and drawings: While ultimately the individual strands of hair harmoniously integrate into a body of hair upon its subject, they do so with maximum differentiation and distinctiveness of direction. In these representations, we see evidence of the willingness of the Greeks to express the individuality of the human subject; the subject is a whole in itself as is the Eastern subject, but need not seek to harmonious reintegration with all other bodies into an enclosed world order. The Greek subjects that I encountered in that gallery represent an extension of the human freedom along paths that previous civilizations were not able to contemplate.

Africa

I now leave the Greek and Roman section and enter the African room. Perhaps the most interesting art in this gallery were the ritual masks, particularly those that were made of combinations of wood, cloth, hair, and other materials. I found the linear and angular relations that existed in these art forms exercised a far greater degree of freedom than was possible in Greek art.

Sub-Saharan Africans, Egyptians, Indians, Greeks and all other cultures initially attributed to gods and supernatural beings the forces that were responsible for movement in the world. As powerful as the Greek gods were, however, even their power was limited by the fact that they allowed their power to move to be subject to aesthetic principles that were founded upon an underlying logic that was derived by applying reason to the quest for idealized form. This was partly out of vanity – reason imposes an aesthetic order that is equated with the beautiful and the Greek gods wanted to be the most beautiful of all beings. They used the fact of their physically perfect forms to assert their superiority over mere humans without recognizing that in so doing they constrained themselves by the set of aesthetic rules imposed upon them by the human mind.

Unlike the Greek gods, African gods had no need for the strict conformity of their bodies and movements to the absolute requirements of beauty. They did not allow vanity to restrict their movements as did the gods of the Greeks, Hindus and other civilizations. The only god that would prove wilier than the African gods was the Jewish god, who forbade any representation that might act as a constraint upon his power.

While non-African societies also began their art with the representation of the mysterious forces behind the manifestation of the real-world objects rather than real-world objects themselves, African artists deviated far less over the millennia from their quest to represent the hidden forces of the world. They refined these abilities to a degree unparalleled in the world until their discovery by Europeans at the dawn of modernism. There exists the same degree of control over individual lines of force as was the goal in the East and the West, but the object of knowledge remained beyond that which was expressed in the world. The artists consequently achieve a degree of liberation in their positioning of materials in relation to each other that indeed surpasses that of the Greeks. In the process, they are able to engage in an exploration of the depths of human consciousness wherein they reach its darkest corners long before consciousness became an object of knowledge in the West.

I found that the strands of hair in African masks most powerfully demonstrated the mastery by African artists to individualize very minute and densely concentrated curved lines of force in a manner that preserved the uniqueness of each strand but also managed to integrate each into an overall form. The expertise of the artist commanded that the viewer accept the ultimate unity and integrity of the complete work even though it seemed to violate every aesthetic norm that governed the presentation of form in the previous galleries. The African artists in this manner managed to surpass even the Greeks in the quest for liberated movement by generating forms that were beyond the abilities of Greek artists to incorporate into their works. Western aesthetics would have to evolve for over twenty-five hundred years after the age of Classical Greece for the incorporation of the African form to occur.

The African art forms thus exposed the limitations of movement inherent in Egyptian, Eastern and Western art. The Egyptian art was two-dimensional, and while the Eastern art added a third dimension, curvature, and was far more nuanced than Egyptian art, it was nonetheless constrained within a closed, curved space, regardless of the intricate harmony that it could achieve within that space. Greek art broke free of enclosed space, but it nonetheless kept the viewer connected to the surface world, the world of senses and materials. Only the African art could penetrate beneath the exterior world and probe the depths of both viewed objects and viewing subject. It could do so only because it had never fully submitted to the aesthetic constraints imposed upon exterior material relations by other cultures. For this reason, African artists were able to connect to a world in the deepest recesses of consciousness, beyond a reality constrained by formal aesthetics by which objects in the world are organized. Because of its distinctiveness, the African aesthetic offers a greater degree of freedom of movement than that obtained even by the Greeks.

Conclusion

A series of galleries at the Carnegie Museum of art in Pittsburg allowed me a concise walk through the ages in a meditation upon the evolution of culture and form. The short walk and yet lengthy excursion through history revealed a progression towards ever freer forms of movement. The placement of the African art beyond the Greek art and before the modern art made conceptual sense to the degree that the African art expressed movement and lines of force along dimensions not expressed in either the Greek art or any Western art that followed it until the modern art period. African art achieved such liberation, however, precisely because of the reluctance of African artists to completely subject the African form to the increasingly refined constraints that were illustrated in the preceding galleries.

The placement of the African art after the Greek art and not before the Egyptian also highlights the ironies inherent in the world's response to the African aesthetic tradition and to Africa in general. Africa is the birthplace of humankind. Humanity moved upwards, probably along the Nile and towards the Middle East, where the first "civilizations" arose. Ancient Egyptian civilization represents one of humankind's pinnacles of that process. Metaphorically, the forms expressed in African art represent precisely the unpredictable, chaotic movements of unconstrained forces and spirits that Middle Eastern and Egyptian societies were attempting to escape when they imposed their rigid order upon the world.

While Egyptian art forms reveal the desire to escape the forces of chaos through the imposition of formal order upon human and material relations, African masks and sculptures reveal an adherence to a quest for liberation that emphasizes embracing and reproducing in material form those same absolutely liberated and hence ever-unpredictable forces that buffet the human subject. The idealized human form is thus not one that stands tall and rigid against the chaos, nor does it conform itself to predictable, repetitive forms in an ultimately harmonized universe. The idealized human subject in African culture maintains a form that allows it to interact most freely with the chaotic forces that move the world. The irony of the African form thus becomes that it is envied because it is most liberated and at the same time despised because it remains so absolutely unconstrained.

---

[i]Weber, Max. "Art and Cultural Rationalization." in *The Sociology of Art*. Jeremy Tanner ed. 2003. Routledge. New York. pp. 46-54.

[ii]Ibid., p. 50.

3

The Mechanics of "Up"

Many years ago, when I began exploring the meaning of Buddhism, I ran across a very simple story about Buddha that I have since been unable to locate or verify again, but which nonetheless resonated with me through the years. The story was that Buddha once went into a very long, deep mediation and upon coming out of it, he uttered three words: "Trees grow up." The statement was said to be one of the most profound that Buddha has ever uttered. I have come back to that statement many times over the years as I have attempted, like Buddha, to understand the nature of being, life, and my relation to it all. In this essay, I would like to bring together a set of ideas that are the result of my reflections upon that statement as they relate to the sociology of light.

There are essentially two great epochs of movement that are discernable in our assessment of the history of the universe. The first is that epoch above-described that began almost 14 billion years ago. It is that set of now predictable movements and relations among elementary particles and light that led to the formation of all the heavenly bodies, including our own solar system, earth and moon. Those same laws can also be used to explain the set of chemical reactions upon the earth that lead to the formation of rocks and land, water, atmosphere, and all the combinations of elements upon the earth.

But over four billion years ago, a radically new form of movement took place upon the earth that is more difficult to explain with the laws of physics or chemistry. Those chemical reactions that had led to the formation of elements, then water and other combinations of molecular structures began lining themselves up into long, thin protein strings. These protein strings were composed primarily of four base atoms – carbon, nitrogen, oxygen and hydrogen. These atoms combine into four distinct compounds and these compounds formed the bases, which are like stairs that combine to form the very long but coiled ladder-like double helix that would become the DNA molecule.

The strings of atoms increased in length and complexity until on one day in the history of the universe, they took on the quality of purposefulness. Their movements and relations among themselves were no longer dictated purely by the laws of physics that had previously governed their movements and interactions and these special sets of molecules acquired the power to determine among themselves how energy would be distributed and what movements and relations would result.

Not only did these molecules acquire the power of self-movement, they also achieved the ability to pull other molecules into their structure and organize those molecules so as to increase the complexity of the uniformly moving body of molecules that composed the structure. The DNA molecule, or the molecule of life, thus represented a profoundly different type of movement whenever and wherever it came to be. What we can assume is that on some day in the world's history, at some defined moment, and between at least two vanguard atoms that composed an organized set of molecules, the movements of life became separate and distinct from the movements of non-life.

Plants represent one form of life to evolve from these molecular relations. Plants are distinguished by their ability to use light energy as their source of power. Plant molecules organize themselves to entrap sunlight, convert the sunlight to sugars, which are highly specialized arrangements of molecules. Those sugars are then burned to produce the energy that is necessary for purposeful movement.

As plant life became more complex, molecular relations became more rigid and plants began standing straighter and taller as a consequence. That rigidity allowed plant life to accomplish their goal of pulling more and more light energy into themselves because they could use the quality of rigidity to reach ever higher towards the source of light, the sun. Plant life may thus have begun as an organized set of molecules that were still buffeted about by the forces of nature, but increasingly they assumed fixed positions, planted roots, and stacked complex sets of molecules upon each other in a persistent upward thrust towards the sun.

The more complex plants became, the more rigid were their molecular relations and the more rigid their relations, the taller they could become. The ultimate manifestation of this progress is to be found in the tallest trees. Trees are the epitome of up-ness. If one were to contemplate the tallest tree, one sees in the tallest tree the realization, the idealization of the desires of a set of molecules that began over four billion years ago when that first special set of molecules were stacked one on top of the other on their way to becoming the first DNA molecule. That initial set of molecules has evolved to become a collection of an almost unimaginable number of rigidly organized molecules capable of attaining several hundred feet in height in the tallest trees. The behavior of plant life appears on its surface to violate the laws of physics that govern relations among all other molecular relations in the universe - matter should not be able to stand up by itself against the law of gravity. hence the profoundness of Buddha's perception that "Trees grow up."

The evolution of the molecular structures that constitute animal life also demonstrates organization in the direction of rigidity and up-ness. While there are many animals without vertebrae, over time many complex animal forms evolved vertebrae that established an ordered set of relations between the forward and rear parts of the animal. With the establishment of forward and rear relations among the parts of an animal, purposeful, linear forward momentum evolved as a characteristic of animal life. Therefore, while trees grow "up," most animal forms prior to humans moved purposefully and uniformly "across."

With hominids, vertebrae began a slow conversion from across-ness in the direction of straight-upness with the ideal of the up-standing form being realized in humankind. Most of us are familiar with the images of the evolution of humans from curved spines, sloping shoulders and drooping arms to portrayals of the modern human form standing tall and square. Just as we can imagine a day in which the molecules of pre-life first moved into that arrangement that allowed them to become "living", we can imagine a significant day in the history of human society when an early hominid engaged in that first purposeful action of straightening his spine and held it in place as he moved through the day. Imagine further his first attempts to impose that form upon his children, the deference he might have been accorded by other group members, and the general adoption of the new form by the group.

In the above actions are manifest the beginnings of social class and the early aspirations of the nobility. Class is first and foremost a linear quality. Class straightens out, forces upwards, and balances so that up-ness can be sustained. Class stands tall and never slouches. No other animal groups have normatively imposed posture upon its other members as have human societies. In that regard, modern humans are the complement to trees as the ultimate manifestations of "up" in the world. To Buddha's statement "Trees grow up," I would therefore add "Humans stand up."

The quest for up in ancient Egypt

Early human societies were as inquisitive about the origins of being as we are today such that at some point in ancient history, entire classes of men began to devote themselves to philosophical reflection on human origins. The outcomes of these reflections were often expressed in creation myths, many of which are still available for consideration.

Underlying all creation myths is a similar logic: As we unwind the past in our minds, we proceed from complexity to simplicity and from simplicity to unity. Unity often takes the form of a simple and familiar primordial substance from which all succeeding substances and forms sprang, again, often first as duality, then trinity on the path to multiplicity.

The fact of the manifestation of living, purposefully-moving beings suggested to thinking men that life must operate upon a deeper set of rules that are nonetheless compatible with the rules that govern the movements of non-living materials. This fact set humans upon a quest to determine those underlying rules and apply them to the human liberation quest.

Humans who studied movement incorporated orderly and predictable patterns of change into the structure of their mythology. The most enduring myths are those that "work". A working system is one whose components are logically integrated such that energy can be directed through the parts of the system so as to cause movement in a manner that does not violate the foundational laws upon which the system is premised.

These foundational laws are:

1. An object at rest must be acted upon by some force in order to move.

2. Similarly, an object already in motion requires power to accelerate – to speed up, slow down or change direction.

3. The generation of force requires power. In turn, power requires some mechanism for its production. A mechanism is an arrangement of existing materials that generates the kinetic potential that can produce the willful movement desired by living beings.

4. All bodies with substance and weight will be affected by the force of gravity. The law of gravity states simply and absolutely that heavy materials are pulled downwards, including, most importantly, the human body.

5. All substances, materials, and forces in the universe are forms of energy. Energy can be transformed between all its forms of expression.

6. Energy is conserved. It can be neither created nor destroyed. The working system that defines the world thus contains a finite amount of energy that is dynamically distributed among its parts.

While many of these foundational constraints upon relations in the world had been deduced by ancient thinkers and are reflected in their art, mythologies, and religions, they were formalized in the seventeenth century into inviolable laws by Sir Isaac Newton and form the foundation of the modern science of physics. Within these laws can be discerned the problem that countless generations of minds have pondered, which is that humans have a body that must be moved, that the body requires power to move, that power in turn requires transferable energy, which in turn requires a continuing mechanism to produce transferable energy. If these conditions are not consistently met, the human body will ultimately succumb to the laws of inertia and gravity that cause the cessation of bodies' power to hold itself together as a unity against the disintegrating effects of natural forces. The above-cited conditions must therefore be sustained or the body will die.

As all human bodies do in fact die, the problem remains a critical one that must continually be addressed in all societies through all time. Great effort is therefore directed towards determining the underlying mechanics of movement and then applying the derived principles to keeping humans up, alive and moving. The human aspirations to be and to express will never acquire true meaning as long as all that is created, including the human subject, is ultimately destroyed. Some of the deepest reflections by human subjects have thus focused upon trying to understand the underlying mechanics of existence and the results of those reflections permeate both the ideational and material cultural productions of humankind. As cultural productions, the most enduring myths of a society are therefore the products of an intense effort by the philosopher class to uncover and explain the foundational mechanics of being.

The earliest metaphysicists simply attributed the power to move material objects in the world, including the human body, to spirits. Objects therefore moved because they were inhabited by spirits. From this primitive physics arose animism and subsequently religion. Reason forces these thinkers to conclude, however, that even spirits must have a source for their power. Spirits must therefore know something about how to organize the materials of the world around their essences in a manner that allows them to accumulate a power to move – kinetic energy – and direct that concentrated energy as a force capable of altering relations in the world.

In Egyptian metaphysics, the god Atum was the primordial spirit was the first being to solve the fundamental problem of how to achieve purposeful movement. Egyptian mythology traces the unfolding world back to water as the primordial substance of being. In the world's beginning, Atum, who is said to be the source of all being in the world, found himself immersed within that water. According to the myth, Atum rose from the waters as a primeval mound, then masturbated and shot his sperm into the sky. In so doing, he created air and moisture, then sky and earth, which are all anthropomorphized as his offspring. From those initial movements proceeded the rest of creation leading up all relations that constituted the Egyptian world.

As the primordial element, water, however, immediately presents the mechanical problem of how a being can rise from a perfectly fluid and heavy substance in which it seems theoretically impossible to generate the kinetic energy necessary to do so. Consider Atum's original position in the waters. If Atum had the power all along to rise above the waters, why did he allow himself to be trapped in these waters? If he did not have the power all along, then Atum had to acquire a mechanism that would eventually propel him above the waters and allow him to structure that initial mound. By what mechanism could he do so if the entire world was water?

Atum's problem mirrors the problem of the earliest molecules of life – just as a structure had to be generated among those molecules to capture light energy in that special life-generating way, Atum seemingly had to generate a structure, with water as his only material, which could rise above the waters and maintain its integrity against the waters. While plants at least had light energy as a catalyst, there is not such indication that a similar such catalyst for movement existed within the primordial waters in which Atum was bound. Atum's problem of how to acquire the kinetic energy required to make his great leap above the waters was therefore doubly difficult.

Just as we don't know how the molecules of the DNA stacked themselves one on top of the other to organize themselves in a manner to receive the spark of light that would give bring them to life, Egyptian physicists presented no discernable mechanics that demonstrated how Atum managed in one moment in the history of the world to achieve the upward thrust to become that first mound of being upon the waters. Once Atum was above the waters, however, a discernable working model of the universe does emerge.

After his self-directed formation, Atum supposedly shot his sperm (or spit) straight upwards, perhaps in the manner that a volcano spews the earth's matter into the sky. That force from Atum encountered a disk at the top of the world and reflected energy back down upon the surface of the world. Egyptian metaphysicists thus use Atum's actions to explain the mechanics of how the sun produces light energy: Rather than the sun by its own internal mechanics being able to produce light energy, the Egyptian model requires an external catalyst in the form of Atum's sperm.

With the catalyst of Atum's sperm, the sun can supply energy for the movements of life upon the earth. Energy constantly moves through the system in a cycle by which water is transformed into light, light becomes life, and life eventually becomes water again in a potentially eternal cycle of energy transfer. Such is the working model of the universe proposed by the ancient Egyptians.

The answer in modern physics as to how the sun produces its energy is that the sun's density causes the atoms in its direct center to fuse together, thus releasing massive amounts of energy according to Einstein's equation $e=mc2$. Einstein's formula explains the process by which two masses (m) are brought together with such force that their masses are annihilated and converted to pure light energy ($c2$). The constant fusion of atoms in the sun is responsible for the continuous release of light energy that stretches across the solar system to reach and power life on earth.

The difference between the modern and ancient Egyptian physics is that while modern science suggests that the density of the sun's center was responsible for the first fusion, the Egyptians placed the source of the power of the sun to generate externally in power of Atum. Because of Atum's actions, substance that began as water (mass, or m) thus becomes transformed into light (c) by some power that Atum came to possess. I say "came to possess" because the fact that he began in water and rose above it at some specified time in the history of the world suggests that he did not have the power all along, for if so, he would have never allowed himself to be immersed in the chaotic waters in the first place. Atum thus had to acquire the power, or the mechanism by which he could make an assault upon the waters to liberate himself from their chaos. He had to rearrange some substance – and if water was the only substance, he had to rearrange the structure of the waters – to create the mechanism that would generate the power of upward thrust.

What is the mechanism by which this transformation occurred? While a group of physicists in the 1990s claimed to have derived a formula for "cold fusion" by which molecules of heavy water could be fused together to release light energy, that theory has so far has yet to be fully validated, though efforts continue to do so. Early Egyptian metaphysicists never derived a formula; the myth of Atum leaves us to take it for granted that Atum somehow acquired the power by which he could sustain a force from within the waters that allowed him to rise above them and then shoot his sperm into the sky to generate life-giving light energy.

Such is the simple but functioning physical system set forth by Egyptian metaphysicists contemplating the origins of movement in the world. The system explains the origins of movement, the origins of the sun and its life-giving energy, and establishes a dynamic equilibrium between the up-seeking power of Atum from the watery world below and the counter-balancing downward-projecting power of light energy from the sun (which became the god Ra) above that plays out in the dance of life upon the surface of the earth.

Water and light thus form the dominant relationship in the early world and their interaction produces all other worldly phenomena. Water is the primal substance and light is secondary; a sentient being, Atum, mediates the two relations. Water and light have opposing and yet complementary qualities – water is heavy and kept down by the force of gravity; light has no mass and naturally moves upward away from massive bodies. Water is fluid and its movements are curved; light moves in rigid, perfectly straight lines. Light thus imposes order upon the fluid relations characterized by water. It is the organizing force of the world. On the other hand, perfectly fluid water generates the possibility of infinitely variable expression of being and possibilities for nuance that are not possible among the rigid, linear, angular relations generated by the world of light.

Because of the emphasis in Egyptian myth of Atum's escape from the chaotic waters by rising above them, two fundamental concepts were central to the development of earliest civilizations – rigidity and up-ness, and they are manifest in two of Egypt's signature structures, the pyramid and the obelisk. Both represent Egypt's desire to achieve life and being through "up" and light. The pointedness of both the obelisk and the pyramids are rooted in the Egyptian creation myth; they represent the up-seeking rigid structure that was necessary for Atum to make that initial assault upon the primeval waters that had him bound; Atum had to construct a structure that could penetrate the surface of the waters and sustain itself above that surface, much like plant life required the same rigidity in stacking the molecules that composed it one upon the other in the rigid form that allowed for the ascension of tree.

The structure of the pyramids tells yet another story about Egyptian mechanics in relation to the concept of light: The pyramids represent the attempt to generate perfect light-form independent of the contribution of water. The pyramids are composed of a series large rectangular blocks that are stacked one upon the other to produce the structure of the pyramids. These pyramids are designed to reproduce the original mound of Atum in a manner that allows energy from the world to be directed straight upwards through their tip to the center of the midday sun in the same fashion as Atum.

The pyramids are also, however, a conceptualization of the perfect universal body to the degree that it solves the problem of how light can move efficiently between all parts of the body without loss of energy. Light moves most efficiently in a straight line, so the entire body is composed of straight lines. Any energy that moves within the structure does so therefore maximum efficiency —any part of the body can be reached in minimal time. All the lines that form the structure are perpendicular to each other. These qualities evoke maximum efficiency, predictability and hence control among all the parts that compose the structure. Such a body represents the absolute antithesis of the chaotic waters from which Atum apparently desired to escape. The relations that form the pyramid are thus beyond the disintegrating effects of the waters and offer the possibility of a body's maintaining its form for eternity.

All lines are in the structure either perfectly vertical or horizontal. They provide an efficient stairway to the desired "up" that is the goal of the Egyptian body. They are a path to union with the sun-god Ra that is the desire of the Egyptian soul. Egyptians sought freedom in the power of Ra. They saw the need to acquire that power and hence reached towards the sun. They were building a path to the top of the sky that they could ascend through a series of vertical and horizontal movements.

The seated Pharaoh fits perfectly into this structure. He represents the idealized human form that is best able to navigate the perfect structure of the world as manifest in the pyramids. The three perpendicular planes that compose his body constitute the essential relations of the human form. Body relations are constrained in the manner that light energy is constrained by the perpendicular organization of the electromagnetic field through which light is expressed in the world. The perfect Egyptian body is thus one from which all fluidity has been extracted so that the body can interact perfectly in the world of pure light.

What, then, is the meaning of the obelisk and the pyramids? They are what the Egyptian metaphysicians concluded to be the necessary precursors to life; out of the random relations that constituted the waters, there had to be first and foremost a rigid, up-seeking structure that could resist being knocked over by the force of water and thus that could stand straight upwards against the waters. This was the mound of Atum. The pyramids and the obelisks are the primary manifestations of up-ness that is necessary for life.

The obelisk, the pyramid, the rigidly organized tree, the hard, straight, penetrating male organ from which the sperm of life proceeds, underlying them all is manifest the desire of life to shoot forward from the depths upward into being and life. Underlying all this behavior was the desire to attain more efficient forward momentum in the constant struggle between the downward pull of non-being and the upward pull of light and life. Nothing from ancient history like the Great Pyramids epitomizes the human desire to penetrate the upward realms of the heavens towards the source of ultimately liberating light.

Eastern mechanics

Ideas about the fundamental relationship between light and water figured significantly in the conceptualizations of the world early thinkers. They likely devoted significant contemplation to such phenomena as the flow the rivers along which their great civilizations thrived, the passage of the sun across the sky and the contributions of the river's water and the sun's light to the perpetuation of life. The Nile River in Egypt, the Ganges in India and the Yangtze in China were influential in the development those three powerful cradles of civilization and therefore figured prominently in the metaphysics of their philosopher class.

Eastern metaphysicists also addressed the issue as to the source of power that moved the world and all objects within it. They also sought to derive the underlying mechanics by which this power was expressed, but they evolved a different working system. One variable that may have contributed to the difference is how the waters of the world were conceived in the East as opposed to in Egypt.

The iconic human form in the East is Buddha, and in representations of the enlightened Buddha, we find an Eastern solution to how a reaction was produced in the primordial substance water to produce the light energy that was to power the world.

While both Hinduism and Buddhism originated in India, it is as geographically ironic as is Africa's position on the globe that Buddhism achieved its highest degrees of formality in the Far East, where the Buddhist priesthood flourished most. The cultures of the great civilizations of China, Thailand, Korea and Japan are all far more infused with Buddhist principles and aesthetics than India, where the Hindu tradition remains dominant.

Representations of the Enlightened Buddha show him with eyes almost closed to the reality before him. It is as if he had left India and walked due east until he could walk no more, and upon reaching the end of his journey, he found himself blind to the outer world by having walked into the rising sun each morning. He turns and sits, facing the west, both blind and enlightened, seeing nothing and yet seeing all. While the rising sun may have taken his vision, it shone through him in a manner that opened a truer, more encompassing vision of the world and his place in it. This is the blissful inner peace that we wit-ness on the face of the enlightened Buddha, appropriately brought to perfection in the Far East, the land of the rising sun.

It is the rising sun shining across the horizon to which his gaze is directed in absolute peace and acceptance on his path to the truth. The midday sun so worshipped by the Egyptians has no value beyond a point in the sun's movement across the sky. The sun only regains significance as it sets in the west and shines its light across the horizon facing east, again revealing relations among all things to the sitting Buddha whose unseeing eyes now gaze eternally westward from where he sits at the eastern edge of the waters' journey.

One can imagine Buddha on his journey to enlightenment walking along the great rivers of the east towards his destination. Buddha already connected with the river spiritually, for he and the river came from the same source and now were headed to the same end. Buddha thus often reflected on the river. He noted the deep, resonating power of the waters. He contemplated the water's unity and wholeness and yet the individuality and complexity of the many waves that composed it.

Buddha considered the varied relations that could be had among the components of the water according to the nature of the forces acting upon the river's surface: Waves on the surface could move harmoniously and evenly on calm days with consistent breeze, or they could be chaotic and their movements in turmoil when the weather so dictated. When there was no breeze, the waters could be perfectly placid and in the winter the surface of the river froze into absolute stillness.

Yet while these changes occurred on the surface of the waters, Buddha nonetheless remained acutely aware of the water's powerful, unceasing and one-directional flow beneath. But to what end?

The direction of the great rivers of the East suggested to Eastern thinkers an ultimate union with the sun where the sun rises along the eastern horizon. It was here at the eastern limits of water's journey, not at the top of the sky, that water engaged in the mysterious transformation by which it would become the light of the morning sun.

The primary energy transfers in the world in the primordial world's mechanical system are thus: The sun rises in the east and moves westward across the sky each day. It sets in the west, in whose mountains the great rivers originate. The sun's light energy thus becomes converted to the waters of the rivers at the western horizon. The waters flow downwards and along the surface of the earth, eastward, animating life as they go. At the limits of the eastern flow, the waters are converted to the light energy that gives the sun its power to rise. The flow of energy in the East is therefore premised upon the same perpetual exchange of energy between light and water contemplated by the Egyptians, but the exchange is horizontally directed between the setting and rising sun rather than vertically exchanged between beneath the waters of the earth and the top of the sky.

The Egyptians could not imagine such an enclosed, horizontally-directed, self-perpetuating system in which the upward thrust of the rising sun is generated by the horizontal flow of the waters in a self-regenerating cycle of movement. One could speculate that a factor that may account for this difference is that the Nile flowed from the south to the north rather than west to east, and the Egyptians thus could not conceive of the Nile's water converging to become the pure light energy of the sun. Rather than rising and setting where the Nile begins and ends, the sun moves across the Nile River and never encounters it. Unlike the Ganges or the Yangtze, the Nile River could never carry the souls of the dead towards rebirth with the rising sun. Egyptians who died thus had to reach the sun by their own power. The pyramids thus represent an idealized construction of the mechanism through which the Egyptians sought to achieve this goal.

What is "up?"

Up is light; up is radiance; up is life. Up is that power that propels being forward in space and time - being organizes matter around the up-seeking energy of light and uses light's up-ness to propel itself forward. Up is freedom and as such is the ultimate desire of all humankind.

Life proceeded upwards from water and when it moved upon land, it thrust itself upwards from the earth to ultimately express as the tallest trees. Complex ancient human societies built structures that express their desires to pull ultimately free from the downward pull of gravity and death. Egyptian structures are pointed at the top because they realize that only a pointed structure can penetrate time, space and matter in the manner that will propel humankind forward to ultimate freedom.

Egyptian culture thus laid the foundation for a western culture that would emphasize penetration, rigidity and upward thrust as the elements for obtaining ultimate freedom. In contrast, Eastern metaphysicists attempted to balance the forces of up against the forces of down in a balanced, harmonic equilibrium that allowed them to move with absolute freedom within rather than above the waters of the world.

There exists some mechanism that powers all the movements of existence and an even more subtle mechanism that powers the movements of life. Life holds the ultimate key to this power as evidenced by its manifestations. The human mind has proven capable of conceptualizing the laws that determine the operations of these mechanisms. Guided by a belief that understanding the operation of the underlying mechanisms for the production and transmission of universal power is the path to ultimate human liberation, an intense intellectual effort has been devoted in all civilizations through time for the truth about the mechanics of power. Conclusions as to the nature and source of power vary across cultures with the consequences of variation being expressed in differences in social and material order.

4

Western Light and the Liberation Quest

Western Judeo-Christianity inherited Egypt's desire for liberation from the constraints of the world by the pursuit of upward thrust. In Christianity this desire was expressed in a yearning for a return up to heaven and reunion with God. Jewish metaphysicians, however, performed a favor for the Christians by solving the problem of Atum that the Egyptians were never able to solve: The Egyptians could not explain the mechanics by which Atum was able to generate his first upward thrust from within the primordial waters of the world.

A working system needs kinetic energy, an unequal distribution of energy in a system that concentrates energy in one part of the system to give it the potential to direct energy to the other parts. Water is perfectly fluid and it is difficult to conceive of how energy could have been concentrated within it by Atum to yield upward thrust. The Jews solved the problem by placing God, the source of all power in the universe, "up" in the very beginning. Energy is already in a kinetic state because it is concentrated upwards in the hands of God, so that when God releases energy, it flows naturally downwards into the world in an immediately dynamic relationship between heaven and the earth. The problematic physics of the Egyptians is thus dispensed with (except to the degree that the answer to the question of what holds God up is consigned to the realm of mystery).

In the Judeo-Christian world, God is up and earth is down. God's light shines down upon earth from above that acts as the prime catalyst for all subsequent movements in the world, including the movements of humankind. While human action was originally guided by the light of God, the relationship was altered by an act of man, and the modern human spirit is perceived to be alienated from God and heaven. Man thus desires a return upwards to heaven for reunion with God. These ideas set the stage for the western experience with light.

The western relationship with light can be examined from both religious and secular perspectives, with the understanding, however, that discourses among the two both converge and conflict given the complex nature of Western light-discourse.

Light, Gravity and the Christian Soul

Like many belief systems, Christianity distinguished humans from other creatures by granting humans possession of a soul. The soul is the center of the human, that place where all impressions from the world are gathered and organized. It is the place where humanity occurs, where the higher faculties are centered – reason, compassion, spirituality, trust, and most importantly in the Christian belief system, love. The soul is that part of the human that absorbs truth-revealing light from the world, experiences it, and then reflects it back out into the world through acts of self-expression.

In the soul, the subject experiences and responds to objects from the world. Impressions of objects from the world are received through the senses and move through the watery body of the subject wherein processes within that water-based body transform the impressions into light energy that can interact with the human soul.

Light is still the primary mediator between all material relations in the world. In the Christian world, light became the mediator between heaven and earth and between God and man. God created the world and humans within it and relates with the world and with humans through the human soul. The soul is the endpoint in humans of light from God.

Christian thinkers chose a physical model of light's relation in the world that focused upon determining the laws that govern the absorption and reflection of light from all the bodies, animate and inanimate, that inhabit the world. A body is any object possessing mass and that consists of a series of surfaces surrounding a center. Light energy is absorbed into and reflected from bodies' surfaces. The absorption of light energy provides bodies with the power to move.

As long as the bodies of the world reflected as much light as they absorbed, there could exist equilibrium in the world. The ideal and self-perpetuating world composed of bodies and light is one in which a finite amount of light energy can reflect through the bodies of the world in coordinated fashion and with perfect efficiency. In this manner, the movements of all bodies in the world can be eternally sustained.

If a body, however, absorbs more light energy than it reflects, equilibrium could be upset and a body would begin to become heavier, causing it to eventually die. Such seems to be the case with humanity: Human subjects cannot seem to maintain the balanced absorption and reflection of light energy that allows them to continue moving in the world. Some universal force seems to be pulling humans down to the degree that at some point in the lives of all, they are unable to stand up against the world anymore; they die and the physical components of their bodies are dispersed. Significant human effort is therefore constantly devoted to producing the subject-object relations that would best preserve the capacity of the human to purposefully and cohesively thrive against the world – the same set of desires found in Egypt and the East.

Christian metaphysicists thus addressed the same problem addressed in their complements in Egypt and the East, but with alternate conception of the mechanism underlying movement that includes, distinctively, an attempt to account for the universal force of gravity, which was a taken-for-granted yet unexamined force in Egyptian and Eastern metaphysics. The Judeo-Christian creation myth thus posits a world in equilibrium created by God concluding with His placing a man and woman in a Garden of Eden. Adam and Eve committed an act that "opened their eyes", therefore an act that allowed them to absorb more light than God had originally intended. They could see more than before, but that extra light remained in their being, made them heavier, and eventually subjected them to death.

The Creation myth states that because of the actions of Adam and Eve, the original equilibrium does not exist in the present world. The human souls of the progeny of Adam are afflicted with the consequences of the original sin. The souls of all humans have been blackened by an acceleration of relations in the bodies of Adam and Eve that produced a spark of energy, leaving black residue in its wake. To that black residue Western metaphysics attributed an intimidating quality: That blackness grows with every action upon it such that part of all light that interacts with the soul in the process of experience, stays within the soul and makes the should increasingly and more light-absorptive.

The dilemma thus becomes that the more the being experiences, the greater the blackness of the soul and therefore the stronger its gravitational pull such that it threatens to ultimately devour all light energy in the world. Multiple bodies engaged in the process magnify the problem and generate deadly competition over how light in the world will be distributed. The fundamental problem of being is thus brought into ever sharper focus in the West with the beginning of an inquiry into the nature of black bodies in the world that absorb more light than they reflect.

Christian metaphysicians conceived of the above relations as a problem of the soul. If the soul had remained perfectly unblemished as God originally created it, then light would have been reflected from God through the body to it and back to God in a manner that allowed the being to live forever. But the soul was blemished by sin. It was darkened and is ever becoming ever darker. In its darkness harbored evil.

In Christianity, this fundamental dilemma of existence has turned the human soul from a perfectly reflecting vehicle of God's light to a dark and mysterious place that is often in turmoil, a place where forces of good and evil battle for supremacy. The Christian soul is torn between the upward pull of heaven and the downward pull of the material world. While it is a place that still possesses the original light of God, that light alone is not enough to sustain the body forever. Death eventually claims all.

The Christian soul thus needs help from God above. Only God can provide the soul with the light it needed to overcome the inevitability of life's downward pull. Only God's light can shine into the soul, cleanse it of its stains, and make it again perfectly capable of reflecting light. The human soul is correctable, but not by the individual. It can only be done by God's light from heaven. The light of heaven rids the soul of its dark corners; it removes the barriers that exist between the soul and God and again makes possible the union of man and God.

God had been long aware of the dilemma faced by humanity and he had a plan for it, the first stage of which had been executed through the birth, death, and resurrection of Christ. The plan that he devised was to deliver heavenly light to the world to establish as a tether to heaven that could save the souls of humans. Christ was the vehicle through which God sent heavenly light to the world. He placed his heavenly light into a human body that would become Christ.

In the Garden of Gethsemane, Christ demonstrated mastery over his soul by positioning it in relation to God such that Father and Son could be united through a perfect reflection of light between them. On the night before his crucifixion, Christ's prayed in the garden. Witnesses say he was transfigured: A light shone about his body and his disciples saw Moses and the fathers sitting with him.

Those who saw Christ transfigured in the garden were witnessing the expression of the Holy Trinity – Father, Son and the light of the Holy Spirit between them. No earthly man could have brought about that relationship. No man born of women possessed adequate light in his soul to unite with God. Christ's light could because he was born with it; God implanted it in Christ's mother, Mary. Christ's body grew around a soul that was kept unblemished by the light of God. That light guided him towards his moment of union with God in the Garden of Gethsemane.

The union with God gave Christ power over death that men could not possess. When Christ died on the cross, his body fell away from his soul, but through the power of God's light, his soul and body were reunited and Christ could reanimate his body and pull it back up to life. He then ascended with that body back up to heaven and God. In this fashion God extended his power deeply enough into the world, into the realm of death, to provide a route back up to heaven for the human souls that were otherwise tied to the fate of a dying body and world.

According to Christian theology, the world would not be saved by this tether of light, only Christian souls. The world would keep falling through time until it reached its blazing end, after which God would use the materials from that fire to create a new earth and reestablish the original heaven-earth relations. But because of the God's action towards the world through Christ, human souls could ascend to heaven once again. Once in heaven the human could again experience the full expression of being in the presence of heavenly light and love.

Such was yearning of the early Christian and medieval soul. Unlike the Buddhist or Hindu soul, which was quieted and inward-directed by the eastern sage, the pre-Renaissance soul was always yearning upwards, away from the body and the material world to which the body was bound. The problem of the Eastern soul was that it was off-center in relation to the body surrounding it and meditation provided the means of correcting. In contrast, the problem of the Christian soul is that it is falling away from the body that it powers and needs a countervailing force to stop that fall and lift it back upwards to its formal equilibrium with the world. For the solution, Christians turned to the correcting force of light from God in heaven.

In this approach to human liberation, ultimate freedom exists beyond the set of material relations that compose the world of perception. There was thus little need for Christians to focus upon material relations in the pursuit of knowledge and truth. The true object of knowledge is humanity's relationship with God through light. As such, the work of Christian metaphysics consisted of conceptualizing the mechanism for repairing the relationship of human souls with God. They sought to cleanse the soul of humanity to create an unblemished mirror that could receive the light of God and then reflect that light all the way back to heaven in a re-establishment of the initial set of relations between God and humanity by which humanity had been accorded maximum freedom of movement upon the earth.

To organize the soul for preparation to receive God's light, however, one must organize the body. To organize the body, one must organize the body's environment. The irony of the endeavor becomes that as much as early and medieval Christian metaphysics downplayed the significance of the human body and the material world to which the body is attached, there was nonetheless an intense effort to develop a Christian aesthetics that shaped the material world around Christian bodies and souls to facilitate the union of the soul with God. The structures, landscapes, icons, furniture, art, and body positions and relations employed by Christian priests and monks to facilitate union with God belie the importance attached to ordered material relations with the world as the path to heaven.

As such, the quest for the light of heaven was accompanied by the meticulous placement of bodies and material constructions against the standard-bearer of truth - light. They were all designed to reproduce that original set of relations in the world whereby light reflected smoothly, evenly, and efficiently through all bodies in creation and ultimately back to heaven. They wanted their souls to float to heaven on this light, but they did not completely trust that it would come from God. They still instinctively believed that they had to arrange the materials of the world around them to facilitate the path of light upwards to heaven and God.

The blackened soul, gravity and black bodies were incorporated into Western metaphysics as mechanical problems in need of solutions. Dysfunction in the system was attributed to an inescapable logic that described a system of heavy, falling bodies that were growing in density and hence their ability to absorb without reflecting outwards the light energy of the world. The world was thus becoming increasingly heavier and darker. The coordinated distribution of light energy through the system was presented as a solution to the problem, and in multiple scientific and discourses in both the human and natural sciences, formulae were sought by which a resulting equilibrium could be re-attained.

Early Christian metaphysics suggested a crystalline ideal as a solution the problem of the body. Bodies can be either crystalline, opaque or black. While opaque bodies retain some of the absorbed light energy into their surfaces and black bodies retain all, crystalline bodies reflect back into the world all light that was absorbed into them. The association of black bodies with death led Christian metaphysicists to associate the brilliance produced by crystalline structures with eternal life. The Christian ideal of a world in eternal equilibrium is expressed in the description of the New Jerusalem in the Book of Revelation:

> And he carried me away in the spirit to a great and high mountain, and shewed me that great city, the holy Jerusalem, descending out of heaven from God, Having the glory of God: and her light was like unto a stone most precious, even like a jasper stone, clear as crystal;

> …And the building of the wall of it was of jasper: and the city was pure gold, like unto clear glass.

> And the foundations of the wall of the city were garnished with all manner of precious stones. The first foundation was jasper; the second, sapphire; the third, a chalcedony; the fourth, an emerald; The fifth, sardonyx; the sixth, sardius; the seventh, chrysolite; the eighth, beryl; the ninth, a topaz; the tenth, a chrysoprasus; the eleventh, a jacinth; the twelfth, an amethyst.

> And the twelve gates were twelve pearls; every several gate was of one pearl: and the street of the city was pure gold, as it was transparent glass. And I saw no temple therein: for the Lord God Almighty and the Lamb are the temple of it.

> And the city had no need of the sun, neither of the moon, to shine
> in it: for the glory of God did lighten it, and the Lamb is the light
> thereof. And the nations of them which are saved shall walk in
> the light of it: and the kings of the earth do bring their glory and
> honour into it. And the gates of it shall not be shut at all by day:
> for there shall be no night there.

Such is the world that is possible if relations between all universal bodies are fully coordinated so that the animating power of God's eternal light moves among the souls of the living without disruption.

Secular Light and the Modern Liberation Project

While Christian mystics applied formal reasoning to theorize how best the light of man's soul should be positioned to receive the light of heaven, the Renaissance represents a period when some members of society attempted to shine the structured light of reason more intently upon more earthly, material relations with less consideration as to how those relations were connected to heaven and God above. Beginning in the thirteenth century, some western souls stopped reaching with such fervor towards the heavens. Instead of trying to cleanse their souls, they began to still their souls to most precisely absorb natural light from the material world.

Western thinkers began to focus upon quieting their souls through a reason-driven structuring of the vehicle of thought through which sensations from the world pass on their way to the soul. The goal became to structure thought to the most refined degree allowed by human reason. Thought would then possess the conceptual tools that would allow for a much more thorough, measured and detailed analysis of relations that compose the world. The light that would then be absorbed into the soul would not be the overwhelming rush of the light of God but rather a finely filtered natural light that was separated into it smallest observable parts and scrutinized in thought for a scientific determination of the rules that governed its relations with the material world.

This process generates a perfect reflection of the world within the soul but, in modern terms, in digital form. As the human body operates according to the same principles of absorption and reflection that governs all bodies in the world, the energy absorbed into the soul is reflected from the soul in the form of the human will. With this will, guided by a reason-ordered soul, the human subject can reconstitute reality in the world down to the smallest and most fundamental relations that determine the world's ultimate structure.

Enlightenment humans thus came to believe that they possessed the intellectual tools to discern the innermost workings of the world and to alter those workings in a manner that better sustained human vitality. John Singleton Copley's Paul Revere powerfully expresses these attitudes. John Singleton Copley was America's the foremost portrait painter of the colonial period. He was known for his subtle and brilliant realism, particularly when painting tapestry and furniture. His portrait of Paul Revere is considered to be his most notable masterpiece.

In the painting, Revere is the essence of poise and self-confidence. He should be self-confident: He is a fully realized man in body, mind and soul. He is one of the first generations to fully realize the goal of Enlightenment thinking – a fully free and self-realized individual. No longer were the masses mere subjects of the king's realm. They were beginning to realize the principles of the equality of men, an equality that was bestowed upon them because all the faculty of reason was equally present in them all. It was upon this foundation that the new country of America was to be founded, headed by minds like that of Paul Revere.

The artist's rendering makes it evident that the light of reason shines through Revere. His body and his garment are perfectly and most subtlety coordinated against light. His face is unblemished, his hair perfect, the materials of his garments are finely spun and tailored, all designed to present Revere in perfect relation to the natural light that shines upon his exterior. There is no errant light in the scene; light-material relations are completely controlled by the artist to the finest degree. It is as if each individual ray of light has been uniquely given attention by the artist's brush and their relationship with the objects in the painting are as subtle as is that of natural light shining upon objects in the world.

As important is the relationship that is reflected between light and Revere's soul as mediated through his eyes. Revere's gaze suggests that the light of reason shines through unfettered to his soul and reflects back perfectly into the world. Paul Revere's being –his body and his reason-structured thought – are in such perfect order that the light from the world strikes his soul exactly as it proceeds from the world.

Revere's body constitutes the perfect instrument for gathering sense-impressions from the world. There are no distortions produced by the arrangements of his being that prevents him from seeing the world as it is. Revere is thus able to attain knowledge and understanding about the world, its relations, how materials are arranged relative to each other to produce worldly phenomena, how things work, or the underlying mechanics of existence. He sees the world clearly because he has applied reason to perfectly arrange his entire being around his soul and against the world.

And it is against natural light that Revere's being is positioned. The desire to position oneself against heavenly light is no longer viewed as the path to human liberation. Understanding one's precise relation to the natural world is the source of the power to transform that relation with the world. No longer did humans have to rely upon the power of God to transform their existence. They possessed the means to do it themselves through their understanding of the mechanisms of existence. They acquired this understanding by shining the light of reason upon the world, not upon heaven, and by so shining, revealed the truth about the underlying mechanisms that powered movement in the world.

The portrait presents a Paul Revere fully in control of himself and therefore of his fate. He possesses the ability to wield power and transform the material world. This ability is represented in the tea kettle that he holds. The kettle is his creation; it comes from his hands. The material of which it is composed came from the earth and was mixed with dirt; it was originally opaque, without luster, and dispersed amongst the rocks. It took the hands of man to remove that material from the ground purified the silver and ultimately for Revere to shape and polish had with his hands until the singular true purpose of that material can be revealed - to reflect light on such a refined level as desired by its creator.

Revere epitomizes the new American bourgeoisie of the colonial era. There was great optimism surrounding the ability to transform the vast resources of the New World into wealth. The individual man stood between the raw materials of the world and the wealth that could be extracted from them. The faculty of reason guided him in that transformation. He had but to apply reason to uncover the mechanisms for energy transfer and replicate those processes. Reason-structured thought is the highly polished two-way mirror through which the truth about the world and man's application of the truth to the transformation of the world pass into and out of the soul. It is thus the light of reason rather than the light of God that could unblemish the soul and liberate the human.

Copley's mastery of oil on canvas matches then surpasses and ultimately encompasses Revere's mastery of silver. Copley's finely detailed portrait demonstrates the increasing ability of man to disaggregate his object of study to its smallest bits of light and to reassemble that object in those minute bits more perfectly than it had previously existed. He exudes supreme confidence in his mastery of techniques such as chiaroscuro and linear perspective that were developed since the Renaissance. These techniques allowed artists to express additional dimensions of reality on two-dimensional canvas that previous generations of artists could not conceive.

Artists used these new techniques to initiate an investigation of the structure and additional surfaces beneath the layer of reality in which objects presented themselves to the senses. Through these investigations, a deeper understanding of the forces that motivate the human subject was revealed. Cleansing the soul of undesirable motivations becomes a more complex task than presenting a receptive soul to God so that God's light may cleanse it. Reason had to be applied to construct far more nuanced mechanisms for correcting the soul. The modern project was born.

A compelling relationship is expressed in the portrait between Revere the subject and Copley the artist. Revere's gaze is directly into the eyes of Copley, who is as supremely confident about his ability to manipulate light-material relations as is Revere. Between them they share the knowledge that all truth and power lie between them. When their eyes meet and when light is transferred between their respective souls, the whole of the world lies between those two souls.

Each soul provides the perfect mirror through which truth is reflected into the other soul. Instead of God being Alpha and Christ being Omega with the Holy Spirit as the expression of the light of the world between them, Copley is Alpha and Revere is Omega and natural light encompasses the entire world between them. There is no need to look beyond, to look upwards to God for truth or salvation. Men could find it among themselves. God is not the judge of truth; other men are. Their souls are enlightened by the precisely designed mirrors of thought that are required to produce the ultimate truth about the world and to exploit that truth to power.

The modern project is driven by the desire to connect all of humanity through the medium of light. This contemporary manifestation of the desire is the technological revolution. Light energy, decomposed into bits and reconstituted into experience for the human subject through a wide variety of media, increasingly dominates the modern human experience. Inherent in the direction of technological progress is the possibility that humans will achieve that which previous generations thought only God could achieve – the efficient distribution of light energy through a working system in a manner that sustains the lives of beings eternally and accords them absolute freedom in their interactions with the world.

Chapter Five

From Diamond in Water to
Water in Diamond: The Evolution
of the Western Soul

The primary thrust of the human project through the ages has been to create the perfect body and the ideal set of relations between the body and the world. In the past, we conceived of ourselves as possessing a body in a world of bodies; the universe is a body that is full of heavenly bodies; the earth is a body; humans and all life forms have bodies. Deep our collective psyche resides the notion that there exists an ideal set of relations and motions that can preserve our bodies' cohesive motions forever. There is no real reason for the death and disintegration of our bodies; the only reason that we die is because shifts in relations among our components lead to disruption of the energy flows that sustain life. If we can control body relations in a manner such that no errant relations occur among our parts, death should no longer be part of our existence.

What changed over time were our notions of how our bodies are constituted and the nature of the forces that must be exerted upon the body to keep it animated. This essay outlines the shift in our conception of the body in the West from the body with a perfectly reflecting (diamond) soul, to the body as a controlled set of electro-chemical reactions that interact with a fluid consciousness to generate human experience.

Diamond in Water

Modern bio-chemistry reveals that of the first eight elements of the periodic table, four of them – hydrogen (atomic number 1), carbon (6), nitrogen (7), and oxygen (8), are the central elements of life on earth, as the form the foundation of the DNA molecules and all the proteins that support its existence. Carbon, nitrogen and oxygen together compose ninety-seven percent of all organic light, wherein hydrogen and oxygen as water form seventy percent and carbon contributes another twenty-one percent. Together, they are also the most abundant elements in the universe, as well as the most commonly found elements at the centers of stars, with hydrogen constituting the bulk of all universal matter. Hydrogen, carbon, nitrogen, and oxygen – 1,6,7, and 8, thus constitute the foundational structure of the universal body.

Each of the four elements performs a function in the primordial body. Carbon provides structure and form to the body. It is so essential to functioning that life is considered to be "carbon-based." Pure oxygen provides combustion for movement: Carbon must acquire and burn oxygen for energy to perform its work. Hydrogen and oxygen together compose seventy-percent of the human body. As water, they provide the stability through which the controlled electro-chemical reactions with carbon can occur. Nitrogen is a coolant; it acts as the radiator for the system of energy-production and transfer.

Life is thus most essentially a dynamic relationship between hard, body-structuring carbon, an oxygen accelerant, a nitrogen coolant, and hydrogen and oxygen combined to form water, which is the stabilizing backdrop in which the electrochemical reactions of organic energy-production occurs. In terms of pure number, life is primarily a combination of one, six, seven and eight.

Carbon takes two primary forms: As diamond, carbon is the hardest naturally occurring substance in existence. The matrix that is formed by combinations of carbon atoms is so rigid that the bonds that unite the atoms are the most difficult to break of all elements in the world. The second form that carbon takes is that of pure black residue that is the outcome of a carbon compound being "burned" and its kinetic potential being transformed into the heat energy that is the catalyst for movement.

The problem of the universal body is that carbon burns oxygen for energy, leaving a black residue and depleting oxygen in the process. In Christian metaphysics, the blackened soul is the outcome, which can only be cleansed by the grace of God. The world was not originally intended to operate so. In the conception of the world set forth in the creation story in Genesis, the world could have operated without combustion – without carbon burning oxygen as fuel for generating the energy to power universal movement. Instead, carbon should be imagined as pure diamond occupying center of all universal bodies that allowed light to reflect among all bodies in the world without loss of energy into any.

In the six days of creation, God established a universal body that consisted of a pure oxygen exterior (the ozone layer), beneath which was an oxygen/nitrogen atmosphere (the current atmosphere is 92% nitrogen and oxygen, below which was an ocean (water (H_2O) covers three-quarters of the earth's surface), below which was a carbon diamond center (replaced, significantly, in modern science by a magnetic iron core). The six movements of creation can be understood as God systematically penetrating into the structure of the world and culminating in the process in the creation of humans after extending his light deepest into the earth center to create a deeply reflecting human soul composed of pure diamond. The original crystalline structure of all universal bodies allowed light to enter, animate, and leave without loss of energy. If properly sequenced, the original light of God could animate all bodies in the world perpetually, as long as light-absorbing blackness was kept at bay.

It was the sin of Adam and Eve that produced the world's first combustion. If their bodies were structured as conceived above, their "sin" would have involved breathing in oxygen from the earth's exterior, and combining it with carbon to produce a combustion that "opened their eyes" to new knowledge. This action, however, would leave a black residue on their once-brilliant soul that would grow until it consumed their and ultimately all bodies in the world in death. The underlying premise of Western metaphysics up to the period of Enlightenment thus finds it logic in the Genesis story of creation.

Modern bio-chemistry reveals the dilemma of existence to be exactly that which is can be extrapolated from writings by the authors of Genesis and later medieval Christian theologians. In the processes of life, carbon derives energy for the accelerations required for movement by burning oxygen and leaving a black residue. Its success in producing energy threatens the very supply of pure oxygen that is necessary to produce energy to power the body's movements. The goal of life is the same as it was for the universal bodies of classical thinkers, which is to maintain an arrangement of carbon, nitrogen, hydrogen and oxygen, with the help of supporting elements, to allow life-sustaining light energy to move among the body's structures without fatal disruption.

Ironically, humans began to replicate biological processes with their discovery of carbon-based bio-fuels, which are highly compressed organic materials from life that existed millions of years ago. Just as the ancients feared, we draw oxygen from the air to burn carbon to produce the accelerations necessary for modern movement. Global warming occurs because the by-products of the burning are the union of carbon with oxygen atoms in the form of CO^2 molecules. These molecules are displacing the oxygen atoms that traditionally formed the earth's ozone layer and their opaque nature is causing greater amounts of sunlight to be trapped in the earth's atmosphere. Carbon-based accelerations thus threaten to choke the life out of the very organisms that those accelerations are designed to sustain.

Though carbon still plays a central role in the construction of universal bodies, it is no longer a diamond within a crystalline world through which information, in the form of light, is transmitted through the watery bodies to animate their movements. In the modern, scientific paradigm, carbon still provides the structure of the body, while information transfer is understood as occurring through a circuitry composed of negatively charged electrons that circle carbon and the other atoms that compose the body. This significance of this paradigm shift is discussed below.

Water in diamond

Kant suggested that knowledge of the world is acquired by the human ability to structure thought by the application of reason. Thought deconstructs and then reconstructs into their smallest constituent parts objects that present themselves to the perceiving subject as unity. Western science has created categories in the mind for all the elementary particles of matter and force such as electrons, protons, and bosons. The reality of these particles to humans thus depends upon the categories of thought through which they are conceptualized. Before a photon of light could exist to the human, there had to be constructed a complex conceptual order within human thought that contained a system of categories that could incorporate photons and all the related forms that energy in the universe is capable of existing as. The categories that define the structure through which knowledge about the world is to be had must be relatively fixed in their relation to each other and must integrate new concepts into the system in logically cohesive fashion.

Kant's structure of thought is not unlike the metaphysical diamond-like soul that can absorb and reflect perfectly from the world but that depends upon the rigidity of relations that compose the substance of the reflecting soul. John Singleton Copley presented his Paul Revere as representative of the soul as a fixed center whose reflection back into the world powered a human will guided by reason. Enlightenment thinkers believed that they could completely master human behavior through the imposition of reason as a constraining force upon the will. Kant confined that reason to the structure of thought and it was to be a soul that was informed by reason-structured thought that would liberate the human subject.

Late nineteenth century developments in the fields of biology and psychoanalytic thought, however, challenged the Enlightenment-era paradigm as to the relationship between human subjects and objects in the world. Modern biological theories proposed the existence of instincts and biologically driven impulses that resulted in human behaviors that were not subject to control by the will. Freud discovered an unconscious component of the human consciousness at whose seat was an id that was responsible for the sex drive, which is the prime motivator of the human subject. There is, then, that component of behavior that could be controlled by reason acting upon the will, but there exists also a reservoir of human motivation that lies deep beneath the source of conscious action.

Perception came to be understood as more than mere absorption and reflection of light energy from objects in the world. The act of perception involves the absorption of energy of objects from the world through internal systems that operate beyond the reach of conscious reason and ultimately into a realm of the unconscious. In the unconscious, objects lose their spatio-temporal qualities and enter into relations that are not possible in the external world. The forms that objects take in the unconscious depend not on the form that produced them in the external world; their forms reflect instead the strength of their impact on the psyche of the individual. Object relations in the unconscious operate upon an entirely different set of rules from those that govern them in the physical world. The images, ideas and motivations that objects in the world project upon human consciousness as experience are not reflections but rather distortions of real world relations.

While the unconscious receives structured impressions from the world, it transforms those impressions into perfectly fluid relations that alter rather than reflect the reality experienced by the subject in the world through its senses. Enlightenment thinkers placed a perfectly reflecting soul as the receptacle of impressions from the world as organized by reason-structured thought. Freud replaced the soul with an unconscious wherein the impressions of the world imposed upon it by thought, no matter how highly structured was thought by reason, descended from the edge of thought into an abyss whose internal rules of object relations did not obey the rigid laws of physics that govern relations in the physical world.

In theoretical physics, the Bose-Einstein condensation is an idea that results from a conceptual paper that was written by a young physicist named Bose who in the paper posed an issue that was to be addressed by Einstein. The paper queried what would happen to atoms that were frozen to temperatures that approached absolute zero. Einstein used the paper to generate a set of equations that suggested that at those low temperatures, the laws of quantum physics would take over and the atoms would enter into relations with each other that appeared to defy universal laws of physics. While in classical physics, only one atom could occupy a space at a time, in the Bose-Einstein condensation, multiple atoms would be able to occupy spaces simultaneously. The rules about relations among objects in time and space would break down and there would be absolute fluidity among their relations. The atoms achieve exactly what the Eastern sage desired to achieve in the process of enlightenment - the complete destruction of individuality and the ultimate union of all parts into the One, or the absence of distinctions in time and space among beings and parts.

A similar fluidity of object form occurs when objects from the world enter Freud's unconscious. While the process of knowledge production occurs in the relatively rigid structures of thought as in the frozen relations among atoms at almost absolute zero, the unconscious lies beyond structured thought and imparts an ultimate fluidity to relations that pass through structured thought to enter the unconscious. Within the unconscious, objects assume new forms from which, according to psychoanalytic theory, their original form must then be reconstructed with the aid of psychoanalysis.

Any and all objects encountered by a human subject can enter the unconscious. Because there appears to be no limit to how much of the sensuous world the unconscious can absorb, the depth of the un-conscious may be equal to or greater than the breadth of the material world.

We simply don't know the breadth or depth of any component of human consciousness. We can measure objects in relation to it but we cannot measure consciousness itself. If it is composed of the same energy that all other manifestations in the world are composed of, it is a form of energy that is beyond perception by the senses or any instruments that humans have designed.

Freud conceived of consciousness, including the unconscious, as a form of energy, even if undetectable by human instruments. At the core of the unconscious, says Freud, is a prime motivator that is not a spark from God that moves the being towards the good, but rather coiled energy, an id. The id creates tensions in the unconscious that direct the body towards objects in the world that produce catharsis and thus satiation. The id thus drives living subjects towards whatever material relations in the world yield satiation of desire.

The id is an insatiable moving force in the unconscious that can't be quieted. There is therefore no stillness possible at the core of the being. This very fact prevents the possibility of enlightenment or perfect reflection of the truth of the world. The id's movements can only be accommodated, countered, balanced, and complemented by movements of the body around it but it can't be quelled for to quell it is death. It is the life force of the living subject.

Freud's concept of the superego is as a structure that is imposed upon the consciousness from the external world in an attempt to direct the force of the id to channel it towards life-preserving and potentially socially productive activities. The superego represents the (socially) structured thought that exists at the edge of the unconscious. The superego operates upon the boundaries of unconscious and places restraints upon the movements of the id, and therefore controls the desires within the body that are generated by the id.

Freud developed his psychoanalytic theories at the beginning of the twentieth century in a time when the potential transformative powers of electricity seemed endless. If there is a candidate for the physical analogy to Freud's id, it would be the total electrical charge in a body generated by the given distribution of electrons among each other in a body's space. Bodies move uniformly and in the case of organic bodies, purposefully, because of the extraordinary ability of electrons to align themselves in a system that allows for the perfectly efficient transfer of information among them in an organized chain through the entire body.

A living body is in essence a complicated electronic circuitry. "Desires" are produced in the body when some electrons in the system absorb extra energy and exist in an excited state. The precise nature of the excited state is determined by the distribution of excited electrons through the system. This excited state creates a desire to return to a relaxed state, and the subject seeks out object relations in the world that facilitate the particular catharsis that is required.

Because of the size and complexity of the system, kinetic energy is always accumulating in parts of the system, generating desires for catharsis that must be pursued by human subjects in the world by seeking the material relations that return the body of electrons to a relaxed state. Freud's id is therefore not located in a singular place or space relative to the human subject but is the manifestation of the total charge generated by arrangements of coiled, negatively charged particles of energy called electrons that are distributed through the body's energy system.

The distribution of electrical charges through a body is facilitated by water. Water is the universal solvent in which electrochemical reactions can best be controlled. Water absorbs the heat that is generated when electrons are displaced. It also absorbs excess electrons and allows control over the pace of electron displacements among non-water molecules. Water is therefore the all-important backdrop for all interactions that occur in the processes of life. Water is the unconscious arena for the activities of the electrons whose organizational structure determines the human experience. Carbon may thus form the structure of the body, but all the meaningful interactions that result in experience take place among the system of electrons that are distributed throughout water in the body. The experience of consciousness rather than the acquisition of a "soul" is the outcome of these interactions.

The idea of a consciousness with an unconscious component results from a shift from the classical notion of a formally structured human soul at the center of being that absorbs and reflects light energy from the world in the process of experience, to the ideal of a fluid and shapeless unconscious that has no formally structured center or soul. Light energy moves through the body through a complex electromagnetic field that is generated by the constant action of the electrons attached to the atoms that compose the material body. The charges produced within the electromagnetic field interact with a fluid rather than a rigid consciousness to produce transformed representations of objects from the external world within the perceiving subject.

The goal in classical metaphysics was to determine a working system by which life-sustaining light could traverse through all bodies of the world in a coordinated fashion to not lose any of that light energy into darkness. In contrast, the modern working model of being centers upon the effort to sustain the flow of negatively-charged electrons through an electromagnetic field so that fluctuations produced in the field maintain relations with a field of consciousness. Through the exchange between the electromagnetic field and the field of consciousness, human subjects experience awareness.

The Evolution of the Western Soul

I have attempted in this essay to present two competing paradigms with respect to the relationship that holds between the body, light and the soul. I first distinguished a classical model that offered the possibility of unfettered light passing through idealized crystalline bodies to rigid and perfectly reflecting centers that allowed for the perfect transfer of light energy among all bodies of the world. The human project through the period of the Enlightenment was premised upon adjusting relations between a watery body and a diamond soul so that light could shine without distortion into the soul, then shine back through the body and to its source, God, as a liberating force.

The latter half of the nineteenth century witnessed the birth of the unconscious as the seat of perception, where objects that entered consciousness took upon more fluid relations than existed in the sensuous world from which they originated. Models of human consciousness developed that emphasized the role of energy transfers along electrical circuits throughout the brain in the experience of awareness. The soul is no longer a unitary point of perception and reflection through which experience occurs; experience is rather the outcome of interactions among electrons distributed through the body of water that constitutes the material human subject.

Important in the above-described shift is the intellectual movement away from the idea of carbon as playing the central role in the structure and experience of the universal body to that of the electrons circling around carbon and other atoms as the central elements in the experience of being. Light interacting with the carbon soul or with carbon atoms in the molecules that compose the body is no longer the dominant mechanism by which being is experienced. Rather, the organization and interaction of electrons in an electromagnetic field generate impressions of the world upon a field of consciousness. Even the center of the earth's body underwent a conceptual shift as it was determined that its core is likely composed of molten metals that are responsible for the magnetic field surrounding the earth, the one that makes all compasses point north. The body earth has thus become in modern times a giant magnet and contributes to the dance of electrons through which all living being is expressed.

Within the set of quantum particle relations that constitutes the most ephemeral elements of the physical human subject, there must exist an event horizon where information from the world enters the field of consciousness. Contemporary theories of quantum physics point to the information as potentially taking the form of photons of light that are generated by the displacement of charged elementary particles in the electromagnetic field that permeates the water-based, carbon-structured human form. Photons of light are thus candidates as the information that passes between consciousness and the physical world through the human subject in the processes of experience and expression.

6

Totem, Light, and Power

Origins of Animism

The human quest for understanding is a problem-solving mechanism and fundamentally derives from the necessity of placing constraints upon the destructive forces that act upon the human body from within and without. Perhaps one of the first conceptual questions that came to Adam, a generic early man, as he pondered upon his world in his moments of reflection was why things moved. Adam's body and individual parts of it moved; animals, plants and water moved upon the earth while the sun, moon and even the stars moved across the sky with some of them, later to be called 'planets,' moving much faster than others.

Adam also realized that some things, like animals and other humans eventually lost their power to move. Adam reasoned from his observations that he would eventually stop moving and was horrified at the thought. Adam therefore began to spend much time pondering the mystery of movement in an effort to figure out how he could sustain his own movement and therefore his life. The intellectual history of humankind is most essentially a pragmatic reflection upon the nature of movement.

One of Adam's most transformative (though ultimately erroneous) insights may have occurred one night as he lay awake in the quiet darkness. Adam became aware of his own breathing and that of others around him. He thought about those of his group whose breath had left them when they died. He felt his breath upon his hand and thought about how leaves moved when he blew his breath upon them. His breath must be the same force as that invisible force (the wind) that caused leaves to move and made waves upon the water. It might also be the same force that moved heavenly bodies across the sky. Adam thus perceived his breath to be part of a life force that could move freely through the world, including in and out of living bodies. This life force was the animating spirit of the world. That all materials of the world, including the human body, were endowed with animating spirits became the foundation of all early human knowledge systems; all religions and magical practices are founded upon the presumption that the materials of the world are endowed with invisible animating forces.

Not only do spirits exist in the material world, they also live in the internal world of the human consciousness and are often manifest in memories, imagination and dreams. To early humans, there was no difference between their internal world and the world before them – both were equally real and both were capable of being inhabited by spirits. It was impossible for early humans to conceive that dying members of the clan did not live on after their spirits because these members could so easily be brought to life in memory and sometimes appeared in dreams.

Early humans imagined that these invisible spirits controlled all the movements in the world and were thus responsible for the destinies of the living. Just as breath entered and exited the human body, spirits could do the same and could even take possession of human bodies and direct their actions. Spirits could alter the visible world and its inhabitants in both helpful and noxious ways that could lead to either health and life or illness and death. Of utmost important was therefore to seek means of constraining the movements and behavior of the spirit world as the means to sustaining those world relations that preserved the lives and well-being of the individual and his group.

Origins of Totem

Freud, Durkheim, Frazier and others have all accorded a central position to the totem in the organization of early human societies. A totem is any piece of material whose common meaning is accepted by the wielder and an audience as possessing the power to interact with the spirit world. Its production constitutes the most uniquely human behavior to the degree that it represents not only a primitive conceptualization of a causal system of physics, but the earliest attempt to manipulate the physical world based upon a set of underlying causal assumptions about the nature of reality.

Their initial function was to place constraints upon the movements of spirits that moved so freely between consciousness and the world. The totem mediated the relationship between spirits and humans; rather than acting directly upon the human, the power of spirits was absorbed into the totem and the totem then directed movements of the spirit from the totem in a manner dictated by the wielder of the totem. Spirits could be directed to cease from harm, actively bring about a desired state of affairs, or to execute justice by causing harm to one's enemies.

Totems imposed radiant order upon early human hordes and generated the fundamental physical formula for the transference of power among elements of the social system. Radiant order is established by the fact that the totem causes two or more individuals or in some cases the entire horde to focus upon a single point. The totem orders the consciousness of the group relative to a single point - it directs conscious energy in a series of straight lines from multiple points in space towards that singular point. The combined social force that is embodied by their conscious empowerment of the totem is thus absorbed into the totem. The material that composes the totem acquires power over and above its intrinsic power to move, which, in the case of most objects used as totems, was no power at all. A crystal that assumes the value of totem, for example, while unable to cause movement before embodiment as a totem, becomes able to direct the movement of any group members to the degree that they have projected their conscious energy into it and believe in its power to move.

If the conscious energy of the group is directed towards a central point, the totem, that point will radiate power in direct proportion to the energy that is directed to it. In this social fusion of $e=mc^2$, e is the social energy that is released from the totem as the total of all conscious energy (c) directed to it from each social member (m). The total energy produced can both control the movements of spirits (in the minds of the believers) and perform the more important latent function of consolidating information into a single source and thereby allowing those who control the meaning of the totem to more efficiently wield power over group members.

The totem is an elementary information system. It embodies an agreed-upon meaning whose message can be directed at multiple group members. A totem's information can be sustained over time independent of its creator. It can direct the actions of all group members who come in contact with it in a uniform manner without the exertion of physical force by its wielder. It structures the consciousness of those who encounter it and causes behaviors to conform to its dictates. It is an indirect transmitter of power, a transistor of sorts, between the creators of meaning of the totem and the audience at whom the totem is directed. It is a means of providing a set of rules that shapes the movements and positions of human bodies in relation their world. Through totems, members receive information necessary to coordinate their movements with those of others in the group.

The manifest intent of totems was to control the chaotic forces of the world by absorbing and directing the spirits that were acting upon the visible world. Singular totems, however, ultimately offer limited restraints. While individual totems may attract spirits to a position where those spirits can be given instructions as to how to behave when they leave the totem, there are nonetheless few constraints upon the spirit when it leaves the totem. It can move in the direction of the requested target or, like the wind, it can spread itself to the ends of the earth. Similarly, while the movements of individual social members can conform to the dictates of the totem while in its presence, the further removed in time and space from the totem, the less power the totem is able to exercise over the movements of social members.

If, however, multiple totems are distributed throughout the physical space of the group, totemic power can be constantly reinforced through society. Totemic systems composed of multiple totems were thus developed to more completely structure relations among the spirit and human world. Totemic systems offer greater opportunities for the concentration of power when the resulting set of totems constitutes a hierarchically integrated system of control. The social power of the wielders of totems can increase within this system in proportion to the number of totems that are distributed through the group.

Animism and freedom

While animist belief systems exist around the world, the descriptions below are taken from studies of the Ibo and Yoruba in Nigeria and the Zulu in Southern Africa (Arinze 1970,[i] Haskins 1978,[ii] Lawson 1985[iii]). Both Ibo and Yoruba are among the groups that were brought as slaves to America. Many scholars view practices of voodoo in the western hemisphere by African slaves and their progeny as heavily influenced by Yoruba religious practices.

The religious practices of all three groups are steeped in the animist tradition. While all have cosmologies that recognize a god of the sky, a great creator, or an all-powerful being, in none are those spirits the primary focus of the religion. Like most sub-Saharan African religions, the creator or sky-god is recognized, but plays little direct role in the day-to-day affairs of the group and is appealed to only on rare occasions. Appeals generally are aimed at spirits of ancestors or spirits of those objects and forces that more directly affect the life of the group.

With the existence of so many spirits and because of the separate sets of ancestors that must be worshipped by individual families, animist totemic systems tend to be decentralized and pluralistic in nature. That is to say that while there may general agreement upon the meaning of some major totems of the tribe or higher organization, specific meanings can be attached to highly individualized totems by any number of group members that occupy roles that accord them a relationship with the spirit world.

Lawson's analysis of the Zulu system distinguished a number of separate roles inhabited in Zulu villages for those who communicated with spirits including witches, priests, and herbalists according to the nature of the spirit with whom the practitioner interceded. Each has his/her own set of spells, incantations and totems used to facilitate spirit communication. Moreover, the spells and totems may vary according to the specific problem that is addressed and the individuals for whom it is addressed. Each village has its own set of practitioners and while there may be general agreement as to the structure of the cosmos that defines the context in which appeals to spirits are made, the variability of spirits that can be appealed to allows for approaches to the spirit world that are limited only by the imagination of the diviners.

The variability of animist religious practices is increased by the use of charms. Arinze defines a charm in the Ibo religion, for example, as "an object which, by some mysterious, immanent and unconscious power, is believed to preserve from evil, disease, bullets, or motor accidents, or to make one succeed in trade, in a love affair, in fishing, in catching thieves, in passing examinations, etc."[iv] The charm, states the author, can be prepared "from roots and leaves having real or imaginary medicinal value, or they may contain dried leaves, texts from the Koran, and such strange ingredients, enclosed in a beautiful leather packet to be worn around the neck or waist, or to be put in the pocket."[v] All cultures have such charms that are designed to bring good fortune or ward off evil - cultures around the world have evolved means of controlling good and evil spirits in this manner.

Consider these prescriptions gathered by Haskins in his study of Voodoo and Hoodoo in the American South and Haiti, which are traditions that scholars argue derive in large part from the Yoruba of West Africa:

> To get a snake out of a person's body, catch a frog, cut it open, and place it on the person's belly. Hold it there until the snakes come out of the person's mouth. Depending on the number of snakes in the body, up to three or four frogs may be necessary.
>
> Mix salt with the person's urine and make him drink it. Pray as he is drinking that all foreign substances will be expelled from the body. The person will shortly vomit.[vi]

Both prescriptions presume that a person is possessed by spirits, which in the first instance takes the form of a snake, while in the latter instance takes on undetermined forms. The frog is a totem that is placed upon the belly to absorb the snake from the person's body.

In the first example below, spirits are channeled through the totem into the persons' body to make them ill, while the example that follows calls for the use of totems to get the evil spirit out of the body:

> To make someone ill: Obtain a piece of the intended victim's hair and a piece of his clothing. Write the person's name and age on a piece of parchment and put all three items in a bag with some grave-yard dust. Bury the bag under the person's doorstep. The victim will lose all his energy and never regain it as long as the bag is undis-turbed.
>
> To cure spells that are making one ill, put nine nails or tacks in a large of water and allow them to rust. Make the sufferer drink the rusty water.[vii]

The forms of spirits are unlimited because the consciousness of the diviner that interacts with them place no restraints upon their form and nor is their form constrained by the external, material world. As such, the believer must trust that the diviner can discern the particular form that the spirit is taking to affect the life of the supplicant and design totems in a manner that allows the spirit to be appropriately absorbed into the totem so that the spirit can be controlled, if only temporarily.

The assignment of meaning to totems and their association with causes and effects allows for the construction of an elementary classification system, however unscientific and chaotic. The system allows for objects in the world to be defined and their relations to be set. They thus impose a primitive conceptual order upon the world that that allows group members to assert, in their minds, a greater degree of control over relations in their world than was possible without the totemic order.

In primitive conceptual systems, however, object relations could not be fixed because their relationship with spirits was constantly shifting. In the above examples from Voodoo, for example, numerous totems are mentioned - frog, hair, articles of clothing, parchments, urine, salt, and rusty water, and these are but a very small number of the many objects in the totemic order, but there will not be found any discourse that attempts to determine precisely what relationship within the totemic order exists between a frog and urine, or between salt and rusty water. No set of unified, logical relations ever evolves among the multitude of totems that constitute the system. Individual priests and diviners maintain personal control over relationships with particular spirits; they never came together as a class in any of the three groups discussed above to consolidate a meaning system through which they could exercise collective control over the group through hierarchical and unified organization of the totemic order.

Taken together, these African totemic systems and their American voodoo counterparts thus generate a highly decentralized, individualized totemic system in which totems and meanings are constantly shifting from one specific situation to the next. The meaning of any given totem never acquires a fixed meaning. Discursive practices regarding the meaning of totems are therefore very difficult to locate within these religious structures. While there may be overall agreement as to the structure of the cosmos, each village and diviners within each village – the witches, priests, magicians and herbalists maintain their own set of practices regarding the spirit world. Moreover, because of the absence of a written tradition, specific practices may have undergone generational changes that are impossible to reconstruct.

To the extent that they interact with the group, spirits may therefore move in and out of totems, but remain virtually free and unconstrained in their movements otherwise. A totem may capture a spirit momentarily and direct it towards some end, but after the spirit accomplishes its task, the totem has no more authority over it and the spirit resumes its unfettered movement in the world. The group therefore remains immersed in a world of freely moving spirits whose behavior is ever unpredictable and subject to minimal and temporary control.

Judaic totemic systems

Early societies fixed a limited number of relations among objects in the world through the totemic order. As societies advanced in conceptual complexity, more objects in the world were absorbed into the totemic order and their relations among each other became more fixed and thus more subject to systemic logical discourse. It was suggested above that totemic systems are information systems, and information systems can exist in a range between two extremes – either information (spirits) move through the system with no restraints or information (spirits) move through the system completely restrained. The three totemic systems above are examples of the fewest restraints being placed upon the spirit world by the totemic order. The Jewish order in many regards represents the opposite extreme. The point of the consolidation of power under a single God and the worship of that God as the origin of all things was a negation of the natural inclinations of groups towards animist systems that allowed for the worship of many different spirits. Jews, like the Egyptians and other groups, saw an advantage in organizing the totemic system and the spirits to which they referred under a singular spirit or being.

Ancestor worship did not cease under the Jews: Moses, Abraham and Isaac lived on as spirits in heaven and there was a world of angels that surrounded God and did God's bidding in the world. What changed was the structure of the spirit world: God assumed complete control of the ancestors and organized them in his spiritual realm. The ancestors no longer had power that they could exert in the world of the living; all power from the spiritual world was consolidated in God. Any appeals to the spirits would be as intercessors to God. The creator that Ibo, Yoruba and Zulu religions had relegated to the background as a powerful spirit but that nonetheless controlled little of the day-to-day affairs of the group was elevated to central importance in the Jewish religious system.

The organization of all religious practices thus centered on God and only God. All totems that supported the religious order were organized around a central focus, with that focus being the holiest point in the world, the central totem in the central shrine of the people. That holiest of all spots that was to be the direct means by which the people communicated with God through the interaction of the totem with God's spirit.

Consider the following passage from Leviticus:

And Moses said unto the congregation, This [is] the thing which the LORD commanded to be done.
And Moses brought Aaron and his sons, and washed them with water.

And he put upon him the coat, and girded him with the girdle, and clothed him with the robe, and put the ephod upon him, and he girded him with the curious girdle of the ephod, and bound [it] unto him therewith.

And he put the breastplate upon him: also he put in the breastplate the Urim and the Thummim.

And he put the mitre upon his head; also upon the mitre, [even] upon his forefront, did he put the golden plate, the holy crown; as the LORD commanded Moses.

And Moses took the anointing oil, and anointed the tabernacle and all that [was] therein, and sanctified them.

And he sprinkled thereof upon the altar seven times, and anointed the altar and all his vessels, both the laver and his foot, to sanctify them.

And he poured of the anointing oil upon Aaron's head, and anointed him, to sanctify him.

And Moses brought Aaron's sons, and put coats upon them, and girded them with girdles, and put bonnets upon them; as the LORD commanded Moses.

And he brought the bullock for the sin offering: and Aaron and his sons laid their hands upon the head of the bullock for the sin offering.

And he slew [it]; and Moses took the blood, and put [it] upon the horns of the altar round about with his finger, and purified the altar, and poured the blood at the bottom of the altar, and sanctified it, to make reconciliation upon it.

And he took all the fat that [was] upon the inwards, and the caul [above] the liver, and the two kidneys, and their fat, and Moses burned [it] upon the altar.

But the bullock, and his hide, his flesh, and his dung, he burnt with fire without the camp; as the LORD commanded Moses.

Significant about this passage is the number of totems whose relations become fixed by the passage: water, a coat, a girdle, a gobe, ephod, breastplates, crown, anointing oil, an altar, bonnets, a bullock, the blood, caul, kidneys, and fat of the bullock, as well as its hide and dung. Throughout the entire book of Leviticus, many objects that constitute the material culture of the Jews are organized within the totemic system and their relations are fixed regarding other all other objects in the system. All are centered on a shrine and an altar, and that altar, like the shrine and alter of all religions, is the holiest spot in the group's territory.

Neither the placement of objects within the totemic order nor the assignment of any meaning to totems is left to chance or the whims of individual priests. The system establishes a set of dialectical practices through which the meaning of each totem and its relation to all other totems in the system is negotiated among the priesthood in a continuing series of logical arguments and counterarguments. Any attempt by a priest to deviate from the totemic order is branded as heretical and the priest and any who followed him are subject to punishment by the group.

This system constitutes the opposite extreme of totemic orders in which the determination of which cultural objects are assigned totemic meaning is left to individual priests and other diviners often with no attempt to coordinate the meanings within a logically consistent conceptual system. It is very difficult to conceive of a concept of heresy in such a system because the ability to determine the meaning of a totem resides individuals who need not justify their meanings to others.

The Jewish system entails another shift in the function of totems, from one of controlling the behavior of spirits to that of controlling the behavior of living group members. "Sin" was first mentioned in the second chapter of the book Genesis in the story of Cain and Abel. It is a concept that is directed at the behavior of the group rather than that of the spirit world. Throughout Leviticus are prescriptions regarding the behavior of group members in the areas of cleanliness, marital relations, and the requirements of purification.

In the Book of Leviticus, one can sense the beginnings of an obsession with cleanliness and the need for purification.[viii] Inherent in these practices is an evolving idea that perhaps illness and death are not caused by evil spirits but rather by filth and social disorder. Germs and bacteria would not be discovered for thousands of years after Leviticus was written, but already in place is the idea that yes, the spirit can heal, but it is a singular spirit from God, and for that spirit to perform its work, the vessel that it enters must first be purified. The bullock that is offered as sacrifice must be "unblemished." The soul must be free from sin. The body must be washed. The body must be free of sores or marks of uncleanness. Within these practices evolves the idea of the body as totem within a system of totems, and all must be cleaned and organized for presentation to the spirit of God.

Leviticus reveals a shift in emphasis to placing constraints upon the living members of the social body rather than the spirits that surround the group. While on the surface of the prescriptions is the idea that social body must be properly cleaned and organized for the spirit of God to move among it, beneath the calls to God for healing and salvation are practical considerations that stem from the observations that cleanliness and order in and of themselves extend life and health independent of the work of the spirit. In contrast, the overriding concerns in indigenous religious practices continue to focus on controlling the invisible spirits that are presumed to be the cause of disease and death. Animist groups remain dominated by a worldview that emphasizes unconstrained spirits as the prime movers of the world. Relatively fewer and less minutely organized practices tend to develop within animist groups that also constrain relations between the body and the world to ward off disease and death.

Jewish religious practices are accompanied by large quantities of totems. There are many ceremonies throughout the Jewish calendar that all operate as mechanisms for exerting increasing control over the bodily movements of members of the group. The Sabbath as a day of rest is one such basic constraint on the body; it contains many prohibitions as to what a body cannot do on that holy days. Leviticus sets forth a calendar that controls the movements of group members over a course of years, each filled with specific behavioral requirements. Anyone familiar with the Jewish religion will be aware that accompanying the Jewish holy calendar are many totemic devices that are used to mark the celebrations. These devices elicit some form of response from all who encounter their presence. They serve therefore as coordinators of the behaviors of all group members who have internalized their meanings.

While Jewish totemic systems are presented as an example of a totemic order consisting of multiple totems in fixed relations, the same conclusions may be drawn for other major world religious systems:

While most totemic systems, such as those of Hindu, ancient Greek, Roman and many other societies through history, may still contain animist elements that support countless minor spirits, there is also an overarching logically defined and maintained system of significant spirits and totems that are often held into place by discursive practices of an organized priesthood. These totemic systems serve to sustain and coordinate the movements among the large numbers of social units for maintaining society-wide solidarity.

The Totemic Body

The body of the priest is a totem. Most religions have priests who wear special garments and masks through which their power is exercised. Spirits move through material totems, but they also move through the body of the priest. Since the spirits have no form and can interact with every point on and within the body of the priest, the priest may need to be very flexible regarding how he positions his body, his garments and masks because the spirits may use them for recognition to determine whose body to interact with. His mouth and other parts of his body must also be receptive for the spirit may want to embody and express itself through the priest. Many religious ceremonies in early human societies therefore emphasize a great deal of movement by the priests in the form of dances, constant chants, trance-like behavior. The masks often assume odd, often bizarre and otherworldly forms in the attempt to entice and capture the constantly shifting forms of the spirit world.

As societies matured, however, the movements of priests slowed down and became more ordered and predictable. They began walking in straight lines and in processions. The motions and arrangements of their shoulders, hands and other body parts assumed linear and symmetrical forms. They shed the masks and their visages became more human-like. Consider the Catholic procession: Significant in the ceremony is the organization of the social bodies that compose the group. If we look down on the congregation from above, we can see evidence of a social order far removed from the randomly positioned bodies of the earliest human hordes as they perhaps gazed uniformly upon the first totems.

In the Catholic ceremony is an emphasis on linearity of movement and symmetrical order. Before congregants enter the church, their movements and body positioning relative to each other are relatively unstructured. The entry into the doors of the church imposes linear order upon the group. They enter building and walk along the aisle of the church along which are rows of pews extending at perpendicular angles relative to the aisle. Congregants enter one of the pews to the right or left. After they are seated, the priests enter in a procession down the aisle carrying the totems that define the group. They proceed to the front of the church, where there is an altar in the center. They move behind the altar and stand facing the congregation. They then place the holiest totems in the center of the altar and proceed to carry out the purification ceremonies before presenting their totems to God.

The totems in the Catholic ceremony are containers of wine and bread. The wine and bread are the centerpieces of the ceremony. During some portion of the ceremony, the priest conducts rituals that cause all eyes in the church to focus upon the bread and wine. All the psychic power of the group is absorbed into the wine and bread. This psychic power, combined with utterances from the priests, generates a force that can send that combined energy upwards in the direction of God.

In the communion ceremony, the Catholic priest raises the containers holding the bread and wine only after all congregants have been duly organized in the church relative to the most holy totems. Their organization is noteworthy for their linearity – all congregants are positioned in a series of rows that are perpendicular to the center aisle through which all enter and that divides the structure into to symmetrical halves. All their conscious energy so organized is directed towards the totems, and that combined energy is directed through the totem straight upwards towards God, whom Catholics have chosen as the ultimate source of the human soul.

The group seeks to access God in the same manner as electron circuits access consciousness – through an organized physical distribution of congregants in space that allows their collective energy to be refined upon the point that yields entry into the realm of God. Everything around their bodies constitutes totem – a material order that directs their conscious efforts to the desired point that is the source of union with God's spirit. When the priest raises bread and wine, they are perfectly placed relative to all other bodies and objects in the system to refine the conscious energy that is produced by the arrangement enough so that it can enter the consciousness of God in like manner that electrons of the body are mysteriously arranged to direct light energy into human consciousness.

God responds by sending down his spirit to embody the totems. The totem, now with the spirit of God, is then distributed among the congregation by each member of the congregation exiting his or her pew and walking up the aisle in turn to partake of the totem. In this manner the spirit of God is transferred to each social unit. The totem is thus the vehicle through which the spirit is absorbed and channeled to achieve its desired ends. The congregation is dispersed after the ceremony to return to their chosen endeavors, but with the guidance of the spirit of God within them that has been transferred through the totem.

While Islamic totemic energy is also directed towards receiving Allah's spirit from above, the Islamic structural order assumes a more radiant order in contrast to the linear, perpendicular order of Catholicism: Muslim temples do not have pews. Congregants usually gather on the floor and bow towards an altar at the front of the temple. The radiant order of Islam is further highlighted by the fact that all congregants at times of the day pray towards Mecca, which means that five times a day, millions of bodies around the world are directed towards a singular point in the Middle East. Praying to Mecca thus too constitutes radiant order.

There are daily pauses in Islam so that Muslim bodies around the world can face the direction of Mecca. These bodies thus direct a great radiant force to that point on earth, which in turn acquires spiritual power in direct proportion to psychic energy aimed towards it. If one were to follow the direction of the prayers to their source, one would detect a totem in the center of a large circle where periodically many bodies congregate and revolve around that totem in a large, coordinated mass. This is the ceremony of the Hajj that all practicing Muslims are required to undertake at least once in their lives.

The movements of the central ceremony of the Hajj involve the pilgrims moving in a circle around a large square structure, the Kaaba, which is at the center of the Masjid al-Haram, or the Grand Mosque of all Islam. This ceremony reveals the underlying mechanics of Islam to be the idea that the intensified circular force of massive bodies moving around a square structure. When this action is combined with the conscious energy of billions from around the world praying towards Mecca, the combined conscious energy of the group is directed straight upwards towards Allah in hopes of union with His spirit.

Buddhist ceremonies consist of long processions of priests and often end in their bodies, sometimes in the thousands, composing highly structured wave-like patterns spread over large spaces. When all the priests are dressed in flowing orange robes, as is often the case, the result can be quite the spectacle. In these formations, there is no attempt at a central point where the power of the group can coalesce to direct light energy upwards. Energy flows horizontally among the body centers of each member. If all body centers are properly aligned along a harmonious horizontal plane, perfect reflection occurs among group members and each is enlightened. The light energy remains diffused among the members' individual bodies rather than concentrated upon a central point as in Western religious ceremonies.

The observer from above can also look down upon the more heavily animist ceremonies and encounter conscious energy directed towards a central totem, but rather than stillness at the center, there would be movement – erratic, unpredictable, and constant movement as opposed to the more formally structured movements by the priests of Catholic, Jewish, Islamic, Buddhist and Hindu ceremonies, all of whom have slowed and organized their body movements into linear, predictable paths. The movements of the animist priesthood remain erratic because of an approach to liberation persists that emphasizes the totemic system, including the body of the priest, encountering the spirit world as the spirit world is believed to exist – as ever-shifting forms. The animist spirit world remains submersed in the chaotic waters of the primordial world.

From Free to Coordinated Movement

Implicit in the evolution of complex relations in the world is the need to limit the free movement of the elementary components of those relations. Restricting the freedom of components of a system increases predictability in that system and allows for greater concentrations of power. In this manner the materials of life generate the forward momentum that is the essence of purposeful movement.

Two extreme systems of movement are possible with all ranges between: There can be a system where there is absolute freedom and thus all information that transfers between any two elements is completely random and unpredictable, or there can be a system in which all elements of the system are constrained and information moves through the system with perfect predictability.

The evolution of religious practices in human societies over time has been towards a rationalized organization of the movement of social units with respect to a fixed centralized totem. While the ostensible goal originated as a desire to direct otherwise unconstrained spirits into a form in which the power of the spirit can be wielded for human purposes, a latent and more important function developed as the organization and the direction of the movement of the human bodies so that the group energy, not the energy of the external spirit, becomes the means for the social and material transformations necessary to sustain and advance group interests.

Just as fixed relations among the molecules that compose the living body constrain the movements of electron currents along paths of increasing complexity, totemic systems with fixed relations allow for ever-increasing complexity by allowing new members to be placed in the system along logically delineated paths that sustain but extends the original order of the system. Increased complexity is accompanied by greater ability to control the movements of both the individual (the social electron) and the resulting social body. It is through this control that group members are guided towards liberation – through constraint - from the negative effects of the unpredictable movements of the natural forces of the world.

The totem may be understood as a social force that was initially developed to place restraints upon the spirit world but that in advancing societies increasingly came to operate as restraints upon social members themselves. Totemic systems evolved that make movements and relations within the social group ever more predictable and in consequence increasingly complex. Human societies upon the earth have therefore come to exist in a spectrum from animist-based social structures with minimal predictability among totemic relations to the formal, linear systems of Western Christianity. These formal systems in turn support the development of a technology-based material order that facilitates advancement of the human quest for liberation

---

[i]Francis A. Arinze. *Sacrifice in Ibo Religion*. Ibadan, Nigeria: Ibadan University Press.

[ii]Haskins, James. (1978). *Voodoo and Hoodoo: Their Tradition and Craft as Revealed by Actual Practitioners*. New York. Stein and Day.

[iii]Lawson, E. Thomas. (1984). *Religions of Africa: Traditions in transformation*. San Francisco. Harper & Row.

[iv]Arinze, ibid.

[v]Arinze, ibid.

[vi]Haskins (1978), p. 142

[vii]Ibid. p. 145.

[viii]Mary Douglas. (1976). *Purity and Danger: An Analysis of Concepts of Pollution and Taboo.* London. Routledge and Kegal Paul.

7

Structural Foundations of Culture: Square Frames, Redundancy and Luminosity

Square frame order

In the above essay "The Mechanics of "Up", two fundamental epochs of molecular movements in the world were distinguished. The first set of movements was dictated by known laws of physics in which the motion of an object is a result of the sum of a measurable set of forces acting upon it. The second set of molecular movements was the purposeful, self-generated movements of life that seemed in many regards to defy the laws of physics and move in directions and along angles that were not dictated by standard physics. Birds, for example, seem too heavy to fly and yet they do.

For the molecules of life to be able to achieve purposeful movement, they must align themselves to be able to transmit information among each other along a line of communication that is inaccessible to non-living molecules. N. Catherine Hayes wrote of creatures evolving "who achieved locomotion by exploiting a bug in the way the conservation of momentum was defined in the world's artefactual physics (Hayes 1999)." There was a moment in the existence of the universe between non-life and the existence of life in which the molecules of life positioned themselves in relation to each other along a set of angles that had not previously been attained in the world, and thus acquired among them a synergy that allowed them to be more than the sum of their parts. This synergy imparted to them not only the power of self-motivation but also the power to draw other molecules towards them and dictate how they should also move. In this manner life increased in complexity.

Like the organisms of life, societies evolved from relatively simple to the complex forms that we witness today. Just as the molecules of life exploited a bug in the laws of conservation of energy that allowed them to move purposefully and with increasing complexity and efficiency, individuals in complex societies began moving and arranging their materials along dimensions that increased their complexity and efficiency of movement relative to the movements of original primitive human groupings.

The square frame of reference embodies that new dimension into which human actions began to be aligned in the leap into "civilization." A very distinguishable human social action occurred when an early human observed a relationship between two objects or a set of objects and intuited that a "better" arrangement was possible between them. Someone noticed that a linear relationship between two points or a symmetrical relationship among objects in a space generated a greater inner satisfaction in them than if the arrangement was non-linear or asymmetrical. Another might have noticed that such straight lines that divided relations within his purview into symmetrical halves offered even more internal satisfaction.

Initially no greater functional value was added to the new arrangements; the effect of the new arrangement was purely sensual and the social value thus aesthetic. Eventually, however, functionality was discovered in linearity and symmetry. For one, linear arrangements made measurements easier; secondly, symmetrical arrangements proved instrumental in achieving that ever-present human desire for "up" since the force of straight up could be maintained only with perfect symmetrical balance. Consequently, at some point in the history of the world, group leaders began insisting that all arrangements of materials and even human bodies be organized within the framework dictated by combinations of straight lines and ninety-degree angles. The square frame that results from the enclosure of space in this arrangement ultimately became the aesthetic foundation of all civilizations.

The advantage of this system is that it can convey information that is easily distinguishable from "noise," or movement out of square frame order. Once information is ordered within the square frame, the rules of balance and symmetry allow the interpreter of the information to separate out that information that does not conform to those rules – information that contributes asymmetry to the square frame. Once acclimated to the norms of the square frame, one can easily see what does and does not fit in an ordered information system and hence rearrange the relations according to agreed-upon rules.

Both life and human society are ultimately aesthetic endeavors. In order that both survive, they must adhere to strict sets of rules as to how molecules in the case of organisms and social bodies and materials in the case of societies will be arranged in the spaces that in which their bodies interact. Properly arranged materials enhance or extend life; improperly placed materials can lead to chaos, disease and death.

Georg Simmel states that symmetry is the first aesthetic principle in the organization of social life:

> The origin of all aesthetic themes is found in symmetry. Before man can bring an idea, meaning, harmony into things, he must first form them symmetrically. The various parts of the whole must be balanced against one another, and arranged evenly around a center. In this fashion man's form-giving power, in contrast to the contingent and confusing character of mere nature, becomes most quickly, visibly, and immediately clear. Thus, the first aesthetic step leads beyond a mere acceptance of the meaninglessness of things to a will to transform them symmetrically (Etzkorn 1968: 71).

Such symmetry, notes Simmel, serves a valuable function when it comes to government:

> Symmetrical organizations facilitate the ruling of many from a single point. Norms can be imposed from above with less resistance and greater effectiveness in a symmetrical organization than in a system whose inner structure is irregular and fluctuating.

Simmel compared ideal socialist societies to the functional aesthetics of machines:

> Consider, for example, the aesthetic appeal of machines: the absolute purposefulness and reliability of motions, the extreme reduction of resistance and friction, the harmonic integration of the most minute and the largest parts, provides machines with a particular beauty. The organization of a factory and the plan of a socialist state only repeat this beauty on larger scales. This peculiar interest in harmony and symmetry by which socialism demonstrates its rationalistic character, and by which it aims to stylize social life, is expressed purely externally by the fact that socialistic utopias are always set up according to principles of symmetry.

The twentieth century was a great failed experiment in attempts to the implement the aesthetically perfectible society-as-machine paradigm. Adolf Hitler epitomized the effort. Hitler sought to correct the flaws in human bodies and their environments that prevented the realization of the perfect set of human relations with the world through which both the whole and the individuals that composed the whole could interact in perfect functioning harmony, and where any desire emanating from him as ruler could be immediately realized in the world.

To achieve that goal, however, all noise had to be reduced, all ugliness erased, disruptive bodies had to be removed, and social bodies and environmental materials had to be organized so that no destructive energy could flow through the society. Hitler felt justified in using whatever means necessary, with an emphasis on extreme violence, to accomplish his goals of an aesthetically ordered society. His ideals, however, originated in the initial organization of all humans and materials within the formal requirements of the square frame.

While Hitler inherited a rigidly organized material order, the social order had descended, in many regards, to the movements of a primitive horde. Great social disorder and mob violence dominated many of Germany's cities. Hitler's solution was to realign the movements of those bodies into a rigid, formal, hierarchically-ordered socialist society. Human bodies would move in coordination with the machines that generated power in perfect coordination. The power produced by this union of man with machine would flow upwards to Hitler to be wielded with his absolute authority. Hitler wielded this power downwards by delivering his will through a perfectly efficient bureaucratic that allowed his will to be carried out on every level of society.

Hitler's power structure reflects the pyramid-driven ideal of the Egyptians by which all fluidity was extracted from social and material relations and the freedom of humanity was pursued in the rigid, linear lines characterized by the realm of pure light. It represents an extreme form of the ordering of all materials and bodies that compose a society's culture within the formal constraints of the square frame.

The application of square frame order to organize material relations was most refined in the West in the form of the Cartesian coordinate system. It is through this system that the measurement of object relations in time and space took on a precision that makes all modern scientific endeavors possible. Movement and relations in space take on the quality of rationality and predictability when interpreted within the square frame. Western scientists began to employ the full capacity of the infinitely expandable and collapsible square frame in which could be measured relations among both the largest and smallest components of existence.

The perpendicular relations that define the square frame in fact express elemental light order: The electromagnetic field is composed of an electric field and a magnetic field, and these two fields exist in a perpendicular relationship with each other – as a force moves forward, a corresponding force will move perpendicular to the forward movement. This fact imposes an inviolable perpendicular order upon all interactions within the electromagnetic field and provides the foundational structure for all material relations in the world. The mimicking by humans of this perpendicular relationship in the reordering of their material world led to the possibilities of increased complexity that are manifest in present levels of societal development.

Redundancy

Redundancy presents itself in the material order as repetitive geometric forms and is an important mechanism for maintaining social stability: An outcome of increasing societal complexity is that larger populations can be sustained. Constraints must be imposed on the movements of these larger numbers as chaos leads to destruction and death. One of the most important constraints is putting bodies to work in the transformation of the materials necessary to sustain society. With increased organization of labor and hence efficiency, however, fewer societal members are required to produce life-sustaining goods and services. Surplus populations are generated. If this surplus labor of a population is not adequately controlled, it becomes a threat to social order, as the long history of rebellions among human societies attest.

The ruling classes employed a variety of means of social control of redundant populations that included organizing them into vehicles of war and conquest, and in times of peach involvement in massive rearrangement of materials. Some of the material transformations, such as roads, canals, and dwellings, served critical life-sustaining function while others, such as temples, tombs, decorations and public art, served no greater manifest function than to absorb surplus labor. The transformed materials could, however, with appropriate symbolism, become parts of a system of totems that contributed to the maintenance of social order.

On the surface, the Great Pyramids appear to serve no greater purpose than to surround a six-foot coffin that contains the body of a dead ruler. On the other hand, the millions of man-hours of labor it took to construct them serve the additional function of ordering and rationalizing the social units who took part in constructing them. The workers that built the structures, the soldiers who guarded them, the architects and engineers who oversaw the project, suppliers, artisans, bankers, the farmers who grew the food who sustained them and all the personnel in all the ancillary businesses that were sustained by the works' construction were obviously useless to the rulers of society. If the labor were not superfluous, it would have been diverted to more significant enterprises. Instead, the workers and the social system that supported their labor were put to work embellishing a grave.

All those who participated in these endeavors were therefore redundant members of society. The workers who built the pyramids engaged in repetitive, redundant actions: Stacking equal-sized rectangular blocks of stone on top of each other in a pyramid. To what end? Their very organization into the redundant labor force lent order and structure to society while imparting to them through the structure a symbolic system that rationalized the social structure by which they were defined. Moreover, if the ruling class had need of them for more society-sustaining efforts, they were already prepared for participation in those endeavors by having had their movements ordered through these redundant activities. The ruling classes thus recognized the need to engage surplus populations in redundant tasks. Such aesthetically-driven arrangements may contribute to or be the result of humans in the progression of civilization having to live increasingly closer to each other and in the small squares of space that come to constrain their movements.

Redundant labor is directed both towards refining large and small spaces. Relations within spaces of definite size can be infinitely refined. A tapestry may be only large enough to cover a single wall, but the repetitive intricacy of the movements may occupy as much labor time as some of the largest constructions of a society. An examination of the architecture and ornamentation of many Asian social spaces from this perspective reveals, for example, an emphasis on the societal emphasis on dividing up spaces into ever-decreasing frames. Bannisters, ornaments, carvings, totems, two-dimensional artwork, and all manner of redundant geometric forms present an attempt to bring even the smallest spaces within the realm of square frame order. It is therefore very difficult to find large, flat, unadorned Asian spaces as the tendency is to assure that all individual segments of space, down to the smallest squares possible, are brought within the harmonic order of existence. This form of redundancy may be considered as either contributing cause or effect of Asian countries' ability to sustain the largest and densest populations of all regions of the world, as each social unit must learn to adapt to movement in increasingly small spaces while interacting among densely packed group members.

The Japanese tea ceremony and all the preparations and rituals surrounding it offer another example of how redundant behavior orders society. The ceremony revolves around the act of lifting a cup of tea to the lips to drink, an act that performs the basic function of alleviating the thirst of an organism. Yet an extremely elaborate system of preparations and movements precedes and are coordinated around the ultimate act of lifting of the cup to the mouth. The tea must be grown and prepared in a certain way. All manner of utensils must be created and acquired in an accompanying economy to assure that the tea is properly prepared. Those who serve the tea must be dressed in a certain manner. Each object surrounding the ceremony – the utensils, dress, furnishings, architecture and landscaping are all endowed with symbolic meanings within an integrated philosophical worldview. The act of lifting the teacup to the lips for consumption is thus a coordinated movement that takes place within a tediously organized structure that allows the act of drinking the tea to contribute to rather than detract from the harmonious flow of existence.

The tea ceremony extends deeply into Japanese society and integrates a host of other institutional structures and defined roles into the act. Schools must be formed to transmit the information necessary to properly prepare and serve the tea. There must also be schools that train individuals how to extract the resources from the earth and transform them into the utensils in which the tea is served, as well as the structures and dress in which it is served. There must be masters of the discourse surrounding the tea ceremony; a group of scholars must exist who are responsible for allocating and preserving the symbolic meanings that are to be attached to every movement and gesture involved in the ceremony. Landscapers, architects, interior designers, tea-tasters, and a host of other activities are supported by the tea ceremony, and all informed by the same elaborately defined philosophy that governs the actions of the consumer of the tea.

The Japanese tea ceremony divides human movements and materials into ever smaller components and coordinates the movements of those parts with as much refinement as the culture will allow. If one could trace the movements of all who participate in the construction of the moment in which tea is lifted to the lips, ideally, all those movements together would constitute a continuous flow of substance and being. These actions serve no functional purpose beyond the fact of organization and coordination of the movements of many individual social units within a unified and ultimately harmonized framework – producing and consuming the tea in that ceremonious manner is not necessary to the survival of the drinker of the tea. The actions contribute, however, to assuring that otherwise redundant social members not engage in movements and behaviors that can disrupt and potentially destroy Japanese society.

Religious rituals also constitute redundant behavior: They structure human motions and absorb the surplus energy of society into repetitive acts that serve no function beyond that of preventing alternate chaos. Standing, kneeling, ringing bells, lifting and lowering totems, processions, pilgrimages, celebrations are all behaviors that impart to the individuals participating information as to the nature of social structure and social order. These behaviors not only structure the immediate movements that occur in the process of participating in the rituals, but like the Japanese tea ceremony, they also generate entire economies surrounding the production and refinement of materials necessary to arrange and execute the rituals. Church-building, art and icon construction, food preparation, and all manner of services exist around the performance of religious rituals.

If we take away the central ritual behaviors, not only may it increase the possibility of socially disruptive movement among those who no longer participate in the rituals, but that chaos can spread among all the sectors of society that support the maintenance of the ritual system. All cultures, however, generate alternate redundant behaviors – sports, the arts, and other forms of public entertainment are examples - to replace the potential vacuum left when ritualistic religious behavior ceases to be the dominant form of maintaining social order. Culture is redundancy; culture is the means by which the surplus energy that emanates from individual social units is coordinated diverted in a manner that the energy does not collide and disintegrate the social group.

Luminosity

Establishing the appropriate material relationship with light is the most important function of all life. It is not unreasonable to suggest that the first true moment of life occurred when the arrangement of molecules that were the precursors to life attained a set of relations among themselves that was able to capture a ray of light at an angle that was never achievable until that moment. Light energy struck the structure and was absorbed along an angle such that it could be passed throughout the entire body of the structure with an efficiency and power never before witnessed in the history of the universe. From that moment, living molecular structures became obsessed with arranging themselves "properly" against light to maximally absorb and distribute light energy through the resulting organism.

The above essays were intended to demonstrate the intensity of the human effort to rearrange the materials of their world against light to maintain the flow of life-sustaining energy through both individual and social bodies. Much human social activity is thus devoted to the production of luminosity over and above the functionality of objects. Its production is not all for vanity: Some members of society became powerful in part they understood the need for light to evenly and efficiently reflect through its surroundings. The upper classes extend great effort to organize their environments around light. The con-trolled flow of light through an environment is an indicator of the health of the system; too much errant light, or noise, and hence "ugliness" suggests disorder that disrupts the system. Significant human activity is thus devoted to producing luminosity throughout the material order – in structures, furnishings, glistening garments, jewelry, polished utensils and household furnishings, totems, artwork, festivities, and even bodies.

Luminosity is often associated with beauty, truth and self-knowledge. It represents the ideal in philosophical and religious quests for enlightenment and is often understood as the outcome of the revelation of truth. It is the goal of both Eastern and Western societies, though one emphasizes its attainment through quieting the soul through meditation while the other seeks to employ reason to yield clarity to thought. Both cultures, however, seek to attain their respective goals by the arrangement of their bodies and environments in a manner that exerts ultimate control over how light interacts with substance.

The goal of luminosity underlies many elements of the societal value system: Unblemished objects are generally accorded greater social value than blemished ones, while there are often social prohibitions against blemished bodies and productions. The idea of "stain" carries powerfully negative connotations in all social groups. The removal of stain, the smoothing out of discontinuities, and the organization of materials that facilitates the satisfactory absorption of light energy through the senses and into the consciousness of the human subject are central components of all human value systems. Intrinsic to all cultural productions is thus the notion that light will be the final judge of the social value of all material arrangements.

The upper classes in all societies exert great effort towards the achievement of utter luminosity. When they have achieved all the other requirements of life, they devote their surplus resources to assure that no errant light moves through their environment. In fact, all upwardly mobile classes attempt to convey their status by the increased refinement of light in their environments. This fact becomes evident, for example, in the process of gentrification that occurs when declining neighborhoods are suddenly discovered by a rising middle class. The strongest evidence of gentrification is that structures begin to reflect light differently than they did when they were neglected. The reflection of light from windows, building facades becomes more even and organized, grass, trees and shrubbery are trimmed to conformity; furniture, utensils and walls are polished and painted to assure that no material within a space disrupts the harmonious movement of light across the scene.

These arrangements suit and encourage the use of the space by people who themselves present their bodies in conformity with the absence of errant light through their dress, posture, and adornments. Through the organization of spaces, gentrified neighborhoods suggest a norm of self-presentation that discourages errant light order and in the process creates an inherent discomfort among those who enter the spaces and are oblivious to the violation of the prevailing light order in which they are immersed. The process of gentrification is thus one among many indicators that luminosity is a social class issue.

Luminous Religious Bodies

A sociology of light perspective invokes a comparative method of difference as a methodology for assessing variations in light orientation across social groups. The method was illustrated in *Reimagining Racial Difference: A New Social Physics (2017)*. The purpose of the study was to test the hypothesis, derived to isolate the essential elements of the "black aesthetic" in African American art, that villagers in sub-Saharan African societies share among them a unique orientation to light that cannot be replicated among any non-African groups. The method involves analyzing internet images of village life according to a set of criteria that assessed the attention paid to light when organizing a group's material culture. The study indeed confirmed the uniqueness of African light orientation. I extended the study to the more esoteric aspects of cultural variation in light orientation in an image-based analysis that I posted to Youtube.com titled "Geometry, Relativity, and the Mythology of Race."

The same methodology can be applied to a comparison of idealized luminous religious bodies that have arisen through history. While the method can be used for a wide range of cross-cultural comparisons, for the discussion below, they are used to specifically to compare luminous bodies that have been produced in Western, Egyptian, pre-Colombian, and Eastern cultures, with a focus on the bodies of Christ, Shiva, and Buddha, as well as representations of sun-gods in Egypt and the Americas. The methodology was the same as was used to compare light order among developing cultures – scour the internet for images of representations religious figures from the four cultures that have been associated with light, compare the variety of forms in which those luminous bodies are presented, then draw conclusions as to the cultural significance of the representations.

Egypt and Pre-Colombian America

In Egyptian iconography, there are no "enlightened" bodies. Instead, human bodies are generally arranged either in standing or sitting below the orb of Ra, which is at the top of the sky. Light shines down upon the human form and arms are uplifted towards the sun either in praise or merely to receive its rays. Unlike in the East, there is no sense of light having an interior relationship with the human body. Light does not radiate outwards from within the body. The Egyptian body is completely exterior and has yet to achieve the dimension of inner depth. The body is powered by the sunlight's action upon its surface.

Pre-Colombian Aztec, Inca and Mayan civilizations also incorporated sun-worship into their belief systems and built pyramids in their efforts to connect with their sun-gods. While no luminous human forms were found in searches, representations of their sun-gods reveal as in Eastern culture a horizontal rather than vertical distribution of radiant energy: Sun-gods that were located through internet searches are generally represented in flat, disk-like carvings or sculptures. The relationship of the pre-Colombian body with the sun in images located exhibits characteristics of both Egypt and the East: On the one hand, light extends horizontally across a two-dimensional plane of being from the center of the disk and does not extend into a third dimension of up-ness. The horizontal orientation of the world thus appears Eastern, though on the other hand, there can be located no luminous three-dimensional luminous human bodies whose light shines from within as can be found in the East. In this regard, the relationship of religious bodies to light more closely resemble those found in ancient Egypt.

Buddha and Shiva

In the East, the radiant bodies of Shiva and Buddha assume two primary forms – Shiva and Buddha are iconically portrayed as sitting still in the contemplative pose of the enlightened being, while the "Dancing Shiva" is also rendered standing on one foot with multiple arms extending from his torso. Like many other luminous figures, a halo is often portrayed around their heads to signify enlightenment. A circle always surrounds Shiva's upper body in Hindu art. While the Egyptian circle of light was placed at the top of the world as the sun shining down upon Egyptian bodies, it surrounds the bodies of Shiva and Buddha, and provides them with the power to be free through light rather than ruled by it as the sun god rules Egyptian subjects.

The source of Enlightenment for both Buddha and Shiva is from within themselves. The flow of the universal waters through their bodies is represented in the folds of their garments, which are arranged as a series of rivers that flow into the body's solar plexus. There they unite to be converted to pure light energy. Shiva and Buddha thus sit still while the waters flow around and through their bodies to converge the center where they are transformed to the light that radiates through their bodies.

Shiva precedes and is a model for Buddha, who was a Brahmin in ancient India and whose fundamental ideas are largely derivative of Hinduism. Buddhism, however, migrated East and assumed supremacy in societies such as China and Korea, and even Japan. In the transition to Far Eastern culture, however, the forms assumed by Buddha in religious art left behind, in a sense, a form assumed by Shiva that expressed his continued interaction with the world as opposed to the transcended suggested by the sitting pose.

The standing Shiva's body extends upward from the world, usually on one leg that is bent at the knee to form an angle between his hips and foot. Shiva's other leg is folded into his torso. The leg upon which he rests is Shiva's connection to the world and in fact is the ultimate source of Shiva's energy – the energy of the world rises through Shiva's leg to animate his body, extending further upward to radiate from his head. By comparison, the bodies of the sitting Shiva and Buddha are self-contained: The water, as indicated by their robes, and the light that animates their being exists within them independent of the world beneath them. The self-contained, sitting pose expresses a desire to be free from contact with the earth, as connection to the earth is what prevents nirvana. In the standing pose, Shiva does not seek enlightenment and separation from the world but rather the full experiences of movement and expression that accompany his embodiment. The Dancing Shiva's body will ever remain bound to the earth from which it rose.

Existence is both light and water. The complete experience of being thus entails the all-seeing sun as it expresses as pure light upon the world (Buddha) and the dance of life that occurs in the flow of the waters across the surface of the earth (Dancing Shiva). In this regard, Buddha and Shiva are not separate beings but two ideal forms of experience that complete a single being in an eternally recurring sequence. They have come exist in proper relation to each other on the earth – Buddha farthest east where the sun rises from the earth below and Shiva to the west from where great rivers of life, the Ganges and the Yangtze, flow to the east in their journeys to union with the sun.

Christ

The luminous body of Christ assumes a greater variation in how it is rendered in relation to light than is expressed in images of Shiva and Buddha. Moreover, the luminous body of Christ is the only human form that intentionally violates the laws of physics by rising above the earth without visible means of support either through a discernible structure beneath him as required in Egyptian mechanics or a balance of forces around him as was achieved by Buddha in the East.

One image of Christ's relationship with light that is replicable neither in Egypt or the East is the kneeling, fervently praying Christ in the Garden of Gethsemane. In the most iconic renditions, his face is directed not straight upwards, but at a diagonal towards the corner of the frame that surrounds his image. The light that shines upon his face proceeds from that corner at a diagonal, reminiscent of the diagonal thrust of Greek bodies in the direction of infinity.

Yet unlike the curved infinite line of the Greeks, the power emanating at a diagonal from God in heaven to Christ's body is straight and direct; it represents the more idealized form of light energy, free from curvature, able to move along a perfectly straight line, thus overcoming the curved constraints of time and space. While the Laocoön discussed in chapter 2 above attempted liberation from the serpent through diagonal movement through directing the force of his body through a series of calculated wave-like movements, Christ dispenses and seeks to join God along a perfectly straight path. In his moment of enlightenment in the Garden of Gethsemane, he is achieving what he was sent to achieve – he is establishing a direct line of light between heaven and earth by which humanity can be redeemed. Christ is poised to overcome the constraints of the curved universe in his union with God.

Light from a singular source external to the frame is inconceivable in representations of Shiva and Buddha. Light in the Eastern world had to extend from the center of a universal body to its exterior. Light concentrated into a single ray from an angle that did not originate in the body would have generated disequilibrium that the Eastern metaphysics was not equipped to resolve.

Another popular iconic form of Christ is his sacrificed body upon the cross. His body is often presented as a dynamic force, either right after death with the weight of his body pulling him down towards the earth, or alternately, with his eyes towards heaven and with arms outstretched as potential wings capable of taking flight towards heaven. The cross is the perpendicular set of relations that define the electromagnetic field through which human subjects must interpret existence. Christ's body on the cross thus represented the purest representation of light in the world although early Christian metaphysicians knew nothing about the electromagnetic qualities of light. Christ's position on the cross indicated that the path to the freedom of heaven and God resided in a purification process that denies the sensuality of curvature in the human body and imposed a linear order upon it that would be suitable for existence in the world of pure light.

Yet another dynamic representation of Christ is his ascension into heaven after being raised from the dead. The expression of this enlightened form is also inconceivable in the East. The luminous body of Christ can often be found floating in mid-air, sometimes among his astonished disciples on the ground below him and in other renditions already ascendant and surrounded by angels high in the sky. The presentation of his body in mid-air in all these representations defies fundamental laws of gravity. Enlightened Eastern bodies cannot sustain a position in mid-air without evidence of some counterbalancing mechanism for achieving perfectly centered balance that allows the body to rise from the surface because of the power generated from within it. Shiva Buddha do not defy the laws of physics as does Christ when Christ ascends upwards towards heaven, but rather reveal an undiscovered law of physics that is grounded in the idea of perfect balance. Of all luminous bodies, only Christ's rises in defiance of the universal laws of gravity.

The center of gravity of his body facilitates the quest: In the East, the center of gravity is the solar plexus, while in Egyptian bodies, the forces of the body converge in the middle of the chest. The Christian body models the Egyptian form and placed the center of Christ's being in his heart, such that in images of his ascent to heaven, he is pulled up by his heart as a representation of the power of love. The heart generates the power for the body. The blood that it generates descends to the greatest depths of being, where at its core, there must exist a mechanism for turning all the blood so that it ascends back upwards to animate every part of the body. In the heart thus resided the power of redemption. As Christ's heart was most pure, only it had the power to reach upwards towards God to achieve the perfect union that no other humans could achieve.

In still other images he is sitting on a throne in heaven surrounded by angels that apparently has weight but is nonetheless held up by some force that Christians can only assume originates in God. In these images, Christ assumes the position once occupied by the god Ra in Egyptian mythology. From this position, he becomes the source of redemptive light for the humans who face disintegrating death upon the earth.

Christ's ascension in the West is a product of first Egyptian, Jewish and Greek impulses towards determining the mechanics that generate an upward thrust through which the laws of gravity could be overcome rather than accommodated. Representations of the illuminated Christ in Christian art that overcomes the laws of gravity is the result of possibilities for movement theorized in the West that could not have been entertained in Eastern systems of metaphysics. To the bodies of Shiva and Buddha, we must therefore add the body of Christ to complete the human experience. Through Buddha, the subject experiences the truth of light that accompanies the all-seeing arc of the sun across the surface of the earth. Through Shiva, the subject experiences all the sensuality the world has to offer through a watery but light-structured embodiment. The body of Christ does not offer a form of idealized human experience. Christ's body expresses the necessary force that Western metaphysics has determined is required to overcome what remains the fundamental problem of universal being that neither Shiva nor Buddha truly addresses, that of the growing blackness that threatens to deprive the world completely of life-sustaining light. Together, the three illuminated bodies express the liberated human subject as one who can freely interact with the world forever.

Hayes, N. Katherine. (1999). How We Became Posthuman: Virtual Bodies in Cybernetics, Literature and Informatics. Chicago: University of Chicago Press.

Georg Simmel: (1968). *Conflict in Modern Culture. Peter Etzkorn ed. New York: Teacher's College Press*. p. 71.

Etzkorn, supra, p. 72-3.

Etzkorn, ibid.

8

Culture, Light, and Freedom

The sociology of light offers theory and method for exploring the light-related foundations of human social order and development. It proposes that the ultimate goal of all human activity is to establish a life-sustaining relationship with light. In advanced societies, classes of individuals developed in many societies who devoted significant intellectual energy to determining the most proper relationship of human subjects to light. A driving force behind this endeavor was the liberation of the human subject from the vicissitudes of life that ultimately leads to the deterioration and demise of the subject.

Over time, the human intellect became increasingly structured by the effort to determine what best organization of matter and light yielded maximum human freedom. That which we call civilization is premised upon the most essential qualities of light - the fact that light moves in the straightest line of all forces and the fact that it transmits as an electromagnetic wave whose electrical and magnetic forces exist at perpendicular angles in relation to each other. The concept of the straight line serves the efficiency function in human societies, while square frames formed by the perpendicular structure of electromagnetism serve as the organizational form within which all human transformations of the material order occur.

A comparative method of difference approach to the social functions of light allows for the identification cultural productions of light-material relations in a society that have no counterpart in any others.

Such interactions would constitute light markers of that society in the manner that combinations in the DNA molecule unique to classes of individuals in a population constitute genetic markers. As such, an internet image from a social group can be understood as a *photogene* from that group. Images from other social groups can be examined to determine whether the photogene is replicable across other groups or are unique to that group.

A light marker, or photogene, will thus be defined for present purposes as an intentionally-produced light-material arrangement by a group. To extend the analogy, all light-material relations produced by a group would constitute its *photogenetic code*, samples of which are preserved on the internet and can be extracted for analysis. This "code" include the architecture, art and other artifacts, as well as bodies, both current and past. The discussions in the previous chapters were largely a result of application of this methodology to various light-related cultural productions. Below, the focus is on the representation of serpents across Western, Egyptian, and Eastern cultures and the meanings that can be assigned to those representations within the perspective of a sociology of light.

Serpents, Dragons and Space-Time

Representations of straight and curved vectors of force in art embodies the human need to negotiate tensions inherent in the relationship between curved and straight lines of force that structure existence. Pure light is often associated with linearity; serpents are often used in art to represent the dynamic, curved force that gives rise to all forms of universal expression. Serpents represent the attribution of forward momentum to a curved line wherein a relationship between forward and rear is established. The serpent is a curve of defined length; it minimal representation is that of a single wavelength in physics – an upwardly curved trajectory from a horizontal line that crests, the descends back to the line, descends below it into a trough before it curves back upward to the original horizontal line:

The Chinese dragon epitomizes the serpent in the East. Serpents can also be found in the art of ancient Egypt and was the form assumed by Satan in the seduction of Eve in the Garden of Eden. The human mind took the form of the serpent from those observed in nature so that it conformed to the constraints of a square framework – the mind idealized the serpent's form. Two ideals emerge in line with the ideas presented in these essays - one of perfect horizontal and one of perfect vertical momentum. The comparative can be used to test the proposition that given the respective metaphysics of the East and West, the expression of vertical momentum in the serpent's body can be found in Egypt and the West but not in representations of the dragon in Chinese art. The forward momentum of the Chinese dragon will always be horizontal.

At the core of existence is extension of energy, propelled by force, into space and time. The most fundamental expression of such extension is a line proceeding from a point as set forth in the first principle of Euclidean geometry. When a line extends from a point, there are only two possibilities – it can extend as a perfectly straight line or as a curved line. The most perfectly straight line is light; the most curved line either completes a circle, or, should it not meet itself, coils back into the original point from which it emerged, with no extension into space. Existence thus occurs between the extremes of the expression of force, the point and the line. All objects in the world achieve their form through these two elementary expressions of power.

Curved and straight lines of force affect the human subject differently. Curved lines render the sensuousness of experience. In a curved line, the velocity changes between every two points, and since a line in infinitely divisible, the subtlety of the experience of the shift is limited only by the capacity of the human senses to detect the change. The curved force, like the unconstrained spirit, can wrap itself around any form and to interact with every possible point upon that form. There are no sharp or jagged edges so there is no possibility that bodies might be torn apart by abrupt shifts in form. Curved lines thus offer the possibility of the full union of the experiencing subject with form as it presents itself in the world.

Straight lines place constraints upon movement. Movement along a perfectly straight path does not allow for the fluid experience of change at every point as does curved movement. In a straight line, there is no real change in velocity between two points. Relative to movement in curved space, which takes place in time, movement along a straight line is timeless – no time passes relative to that time experienced in universal space when two points traversed by a perfectly straight line. Straight lines are thus more efficient than curved lines. Their drawback, however, is that they allow one less dimension of experience to the human subject than do curved lines. Experience in a world of straight lines thus deprives the being of the sensuality of experience.

Because movement along straight lines are more efficient that those along curved lines, structures composed of straight lines anticipate the movement of curved lines, and this quality allows straight lines the ability to contain curved movement. Straight lines thus offer structure and predictability to the chaotic and less predictable movements inherent in curvature. They generate the external and internal structures of living bodies that constrain movements among material relations. In so constraining curved force, linear structures can direct and control its dynamic energy. Straightness gives form to curved force and puts it to work. It allows structure to be sustained through time as opposed to the constant creation and destruction of form that is the only possible expression in pure curved, fluid being.

The most formal organization of relations in the world to date is the application by physicists of the Cartesian coordinate system to organize objects and their movements in a four-dimensional space-time continuum. The system accords an x and y axis to horizontal and vertical lines that extend from a common origin. Convenient for present purposes is if the space continuum is measured by the vertical line going upwards and the time continuum is measured by a horizontal line proceeding to the right. An open-ended space is created that is framed on the left by the vertical space time and on the bottom by the horizontal time line. Within this space, the positions and velocities of objects in the space-time continuum can be plotted.

In such a coordinate system, a serpent is not a body in three-dimensional space, but rather the plot of the path of a point moving through the space-time continuum. The curves of the serpent's body can be understood as changes in the velocity of the point as it moves. As the force departs its origin, it moves upward and forward along the space-time continuum as it moves farther away from its point of origin. If the direction of the dragon is horizontal, the forward – directed curve will reach a crest and begin to curve downward towards the zero point on the y axis all the while extending along the x time axis. As the point nears zero on the y axis, it approaches its original origin in space. While movement in time has occurred, movement in space thus proves circular, wherein the crests and troughs that form the dragon's body represent movement away from and back towards the original point of origin in space. In conformity to underlying Eastern metaphysics, the movement in space expressed by the form of the Eastern dragon is thus cyclical.

A different set of space-time relations occurs in the upward movement of a serpent. Initially, the line extending from the origin curves outwards along the time dimension and upwards along the space dimension to represent the expansion of movement in both. Though it continues to move upward along the space continuum, however, it reaches its crest along the time dimension and begins curving back in towards its origin in time. The time for movement between two spaces begins to decrease towards zero. There thus arises the possibility of ideal movement along the space axis in no time. For this to occur, all the fluidity must be extracted from movement and movement must occur along a perfectly straight path between two points. This is in fact what the Egyptians and the West seek – to traverse space ever more efficiently until no time passes in the movement between two points in space.

The comparative method is applied to the extraction of images of serpents and dragons from Chinese, Christian and ancient Egyptian art. The ideals of movement embodied in Chinese metaphysics suggest that images of Chinese dragons will portray their movements primarily along the horizontal axis. In contrast, there should be found in portrayals of Egyptian and Christian serpents in which the movement of the serpent is directed towards upwards thrust. Moreover, no serpents in Chinese culture should be represented in which its overall thrust is upward.

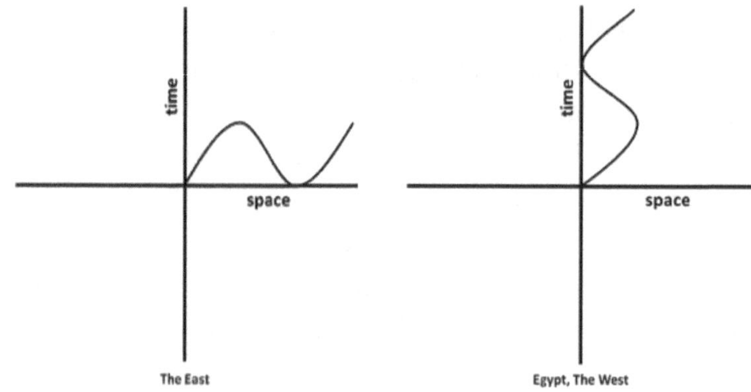

In an internet search for Chinese dragons, the only exceptions to Chinese images of dragons presented with horizontal momentum were those that were used as pillars in architecture. Otherwise, the Chinese dragon comes in two primary forms: One is the traditional image in which the body is horizontally extended from rear to front in a series of wave-like curves. The body has front and rear legs to distinguish it from a snake.

The other common form of the Chinese dragon is that of a figure whose face is frontal and directed towards the viewer while the body is coiled up behind it. The image presents the evidence of pure concentrated energy in contrast to energy that has been extended into space as represented in the previous image of the dragon. Interesting about the kinetic potential of the coiled power represented in the second form is that the thrust of the serpent is forward towards the viewer. This suggests that the Chinese metaphysicians too had determined that an extra dimension was possible beyond the two-dimensional confines of the paper on which they drew, a dimension that extended outward from the paper through a third dimension of space in the direction of the viewer. The dimension is directed, however, horizontally across to the viewer rather than above both viewer and subject.

In contrast, images of the Egyptian serpent can be found whose coiled structure indicates an ability to move purposefully along the dimensions of upwards and downwards. In one major Egyptian myth, the serpent represents the god Apep. Apep is the god of chaos and Apep's realm is appropriately beneath that of the sky-god Ra. Apep is in fact the enemy of Ra as chaos is the enemy of order. The myth thus remains consistent with the fundamental structure of Egyptian metaphysics that commands a separation of the chaotic forces of the waters below the sky from the formal but liberating world of light above.

Though Apep is described as a force of chaos, however, the structure of his body in Egyptian art suggests otherwise and reveals why he is the enemy of Atum. Apep's body is in fact very structured for attaining upward momentum. Representations of his body are as a set a series of loops stacked one upon the other. In these images, Atum's tail begins above his head, and curves downward in a series of wide loops until Atum's head, extended in front of the tail in forward momentum, moves along the surface below the tail. The path of his body is one that has descended from above the surface to the surface itself in an orderly fashion.

In extended versions of Apep's body, there are often series of stacked loops side by side as segments of Apep's body. Tellingly, when the serpent's body descends from above the surface to the surface, it does so in a series of downward loops, but when the serpent ascends back to the level where his tail began in the previous loop to start a new descent, he does so in one great leap. It is as if he has acquired the power to make the leap by his measured construction of the downward set of loops. Apep managed to generate a kinetic force among the relations of his curved body that expressed itself as upward thrust when he encountered the surface to which he descended from his initial height.

In the body of Apep is thus revealed the mechanism that the Egyptians evolved to explain how Atum initially rose above the waters of the world. While the mechanism by which Atum rose above the waters and shot his sperm to the sky may have therefore appeared to be kept a mysterious secret by Egyptian metaphysicians to preserve the authority of Ra, the underlying mechanics of Atum's thrust were in fact hidden in plain view in representations of Apep.

Significant to the presentation of the body of the Egyptian serpent is that the structure cannot be replicated in Eastern renderings of the serpent. Eastern serpents will never take on such measured structure and will never use that structure to ascend along a vertical dimension. The comparative method so far has failed to invalidate the proposition.

In Christian theology, the serpent symbolizes Satan, who is the enemy of God. Satan was once part of God's realm was cast out, downwards into the realm of hell. He has managed to slither back upwards upon the surface of the earth. His ultimate goal, however, is to re-enter heaven and again lay challenge to the throne of God. The metaphysics of the story suggest that the images of the serpent should, like those of Egyptians, express a desire for upward thrust. The mythology often has Satan taking the form of a serpent in tempting Eve and in these images the upward-climbing serpent can be most often found in Christian art. As should exist, images of the serpent exist in which he is wrapped around the trunk of the Tree of Life as he convinces Eve to take a bite of the tree's fruit. The upward-growing trunk of the tree thus provides a solid structure for the serpent's unstructured form to attain his goal of re-ascending to heaven and challenging God's throne. Satan is God's Apep.

Humans imposed form upon the dynamic force of curvature so that its energies could be directed towards constructive aims. Curved force is unconstrained dragon, the chaotic waters, the turmoil in the Christian soul. The foundational structure of constraint is the imposition of the rigid order of straight lines that intersected at ninety-degree angles for maximum order. The iconic form and direction of the serpent in each culture symbolize the means and aims of each society's attempts to capture and direct through intentional expression the coiled potential of curvature.

Conclusion

To fulfill the desire for freedom, human labor is applied to generate the ideal relationship between the body and its internal and external worlds. This assures that the human subject continues its ability to experience the interaction between consciousness and the world. Culture evolved as a problem-solving mechanism through which the forces of the world would be brought within human control and made predictable and orderly.

The quest for the truth about light is a major component of that project. Human speculation on the nature of light and its relation to being has produced a competing spectrum of socially functional truths about the nature of light and being. Each system of thought is the result of the application of analytical reasoning to assess the logical validity of the propositions that are used to support their truths when assessed against facts from the world of experience.

The goal of the present study was to integrate those systems into an internally consistent theoretical perspective through which differences among the systems are ultimately reconciled. Rather than looking for the truth about light within a particular discourse, the goal was to extract the truth about light from each discourse and integrate them into a unified conceptual system. When the common underlying logic of all discourses is revealed, it can be applied fluidly across the resulting structure to expose deeper logical connections among the multiple discourses.

Religion is one of the oldest institutions charged with bringing order into a chaotic world. It initially brought both art and rudimentary principles of science to its assistance. The three branches separated over time and both art and science became their own domains of thought. Considerable variation across cultures exists in the religious, scientific and artistic discourses upon the nature of existence and the means by which human subjects should negotiate it. While surface-level contradictions may manifest among the various systems of thought, discursive analysis exposes an underlying unity among them in the foundational structural qualities that each has attributed to the concept of light.